"The problem with so much person... sarily complicated, often with the ... need. Tim Maurer never plays that ... and—yes—simple prescriptions ar...

—Jean Chatzky, financial ...

"Finally, a personal finance book that isn't only about how to improve your financial situation for the sake of just making more money; instead, *Simple Money* is ultimately about how to live a more fulfilling life, and provides the financial education, along with simple (and practical!) money tools and techniques you can use to help you get there."

—**Michael Kitces**, director of financial planning at Pinnacle Advisory Group; publisher of *Nerd's Eye View* financial planning industry blog

"Amen! Amen! Amen! Simplicity is a gift . . . and this book offers it by the truckload!"

—**Carl Richards**, *New York Times* columnist; author of *The One-Page Financial Plan;* director of investor education at the BAM Alliance

"Once again, Tim takes us by the hand and leads us through the complicated world of personal finance. Reading this book is like having your own personal financial advisor—a great one—sitting on your shoulder, helping you make difficult decisions. From setting goals to investing to preparing for retirement, Tim shows us the way to financial prosperity."

—**Kimberly Palmer**, senior money editor at *U.S. News & World Report;* author of *The Economy of You*

"Some books teach you about money, and others help you find your purpose. *Simple Money* is the rare, honest book that tackles the intersection between them. You can't manage your money without thinking about your life—and the system that Tim proposes can make a radical difference in both."

—**Chris Guillebeau**, *New York Times* bestselling author of *The $100 Startup* and *The Happiness of Pursuit*

"If you've ever had the urge to throw up your hands and yell 'Enough!' when thinking about your finances, you are on to something, and *Simple Money* will help you find it.

"In *Simple Money*, financial expert Tim Maurer teaches us how to literally redefine wealth in a way that will both honor your life values and priorities while simultaneously reducing your stress. Maurer's innovative 'Enough Index' helps you identify where you are today, financially speaking, while also giving you a clear framework for knowing what needs to change to nourish your financial life going forward.

"By the time you finish reading *Simple Money* you will know how to serve as your household's CFO. Whether it's maximizing current cash flow, investing hard-earned savings, planning for educational expenses or retirement, crafting your estate plan, or protecting your household with appropriate insurance, Maurer tells you not only what to do but why it will improve your life.

"And for those of us who love to be given clear, concise checklists, *Simple Money* contains a powerful top-ten list of what to do with incremental discretionary income to get yourself and your family on solid financial footing. This delightful guide will leave you with fresh financial insights, clear action steps, and a refreshingly frank discussing of how to find just the right financial professional to assist you in making the most of your hard-earned money.

"*Simple Money* provides a unique, heartfelt road map to understanding what 'Enough' means in your financial life and shows you how to build a life of contentment and financial security around that blissful feeling."

—**Manisha Thakor**, CFA, director of Wealth Strategies
for Women; writer for *The Wall Street Journal*

"Throughout *Simple Money*, author Tim Maurer reminds us that 'personal finance is more personal than it is finance.' His easy-to-understand guidebook not only explains how to strengthen all aspects of our financial lives, but wisely insists that the place to start is by reflecting on and clarifying what is truly most important in our lives. As he explains, 'Understanding what you value most will help simplify even the most complex financial decisions.' As a result, I highly recommend *Simple Money* as a tool for increasing both financial success and life satisfaction."

—**Carol Anderson**, Money Quotient

"The desire to live simply and fulfilled is the key to a life well lived. Tim Maurer brings inspiration and clarity to the concept of identifying core life goals and structuring the simplest and best financial architecture to accomplish them. His edict that finance is personal is spot on. If you do the hard but gratifying work of truly knowing yourself, your financial decisions will be informed and sensible. There is also a wealth of practical how-to steps on choosing simple, appropriate investment vehicles to support the life of one's dreams."

—**George Kinder**, author of *Life Planning for You*

SIMPLE
MONEY

SIMPLE MONEY

A NO-NONSENSE GUIDE TO PERSONAL FINANCE

TIM MAURER

BakerBooks

a division of Baker Publishing Group
Grand Rapids, Michigan

Published by Baker Books
a division of Baker Publishing Group
P.O. Box 6287, Grand Rapids, MI 49516-6287
www.bakerbooks.com

Printed in the United States of America

Library of Congress Cataloging-in-Publication Data
Names: Maurer, Tim, author.
Title: Simple money : a no-nonsense guide to personal finance / Tim Maurer.
Description: Grand Rapids, MI : Baker Books, a division of Baker Publishing
    Group, [2016] | Includes bibliographical references.
Identifiers: LCCN 2015040648 | ISBN 9780801018862 (pbk.)
Subjects: LCSH: Finance, Personal—Religious aspects—Christianity.
Classification: LCC HG179 .M3544 2016 | DDC 332.024—dc23 LC record available
    at http://lccn.loc.gov/2015040648

Author is represented by WordServe Literary Group, www.wordserveliterary.com.

Some names and details have been changed to protect the privacy of the individuals.

16   17   18   19   20   21   22   7   6   5   4   3   2   1

For my sons, Kieran and Connor—
I hope the many financial decisions that await you
will be made simple because your paths
in life have been made clear.

CONTENTS

START HERE

You can not overestimate the
unimportance of practically everything.

John Maxwell

You may have heard of the 80/20 rule. It is also known as the Pareto principle, named after the early-twentieth-century Italian economist who noticed that 80 percent of the peas in his garden came from only 20 percent of the pea pods.

While the 80/20 rule is not a cosmic absolute, it persists in money and business—and especially in the business *of* money. For centuries, the financial industry has sought to hoard proprietary information for the purpose of selling it at a premium. But as the information age collided with the financial collapse of 2008 and the subsequent Great Recession, an entirely new problem has appeared: now everyone's a financial expert.

The pursuit of money is nothing short of its own religion, and rather than move toward simplicity, its scores of paths have become painfully circuitous. Sifting through the plethora of information from an industry with questionable intentions and a blogosphere with questionable credentials, we're left echoing T. S. Eliot: "Where is the knowledge we have lost in information?"

Simple Money strives to cut through the noise, providing at least 80 percent of what you need to know about personal finance with under 20 percent of the information and investment in time. The chaotic financial world simplified.

This leaves you with a decision: If you'd prefer to live on the hairy edge of financial insanity, this book might not be for you. But if something in you yearns for a simpler financial existence, a more comprehensible plan, or an achievable financial to-do list, this book was written *for you.*

This short introduction lays the groundwork, beginning with four fundamental tenets that link each of the book's five parts.

Tenet #1: Personal finance is more personal than it is finance

This is not a clever tagline but a statement of fact rooted in science. In psychology, yes, but also in biology. The proof is everywhere. This is why people who make a million dollars a year live paycheck to paycheck and why underpaid teachers retire with millions in savings. This is why investors make a fraction of what their investments return. This is why consumers entrust their life savings to salespeople who buy them fancy dinners.

This is also why the first part of this book is dedicated to Planning for Life. One of the ways we can make financial decisions simple is to genuinely understand what motivates us. These motivations are too often separated from our financial planning, even though they are the foundation.

The research and writing of Daniel Kahneman, Richard Thaler, Cass Sunstein, Jonathan Haidt, Daniel Pink, Malcolm Gladwell, Simon Sinek, Chip Heath, and Dan Heath collectively raise a big neon sign that reads:

The way we think people make decisions—and therefore the way we motivate people—is wrong.

We're stuck in an era of carrot-and-stick motivation, even though science passed such a system by decades ago. We're stuck telling people what to do and how to do it without ever ensuring they understand why.

Tenet #2: We need to know why

Simon Sinek reminds us what really motivates people to action in his popular TEDx talk, "How Great Leaders Inspire Action,"[1] and in his book, *Start with Why*. People won't really listen to *what* you tell them to do or *how* to do it until they understand *why* it's important.

The financial industry is notorious for berating people with an onslaught of whats and hows. I'll follow Sinek's example and begin every chapter telling you *why* you need to read it.

The reason *why* part 2 of the book—"Planning for Today"—will likely interest you is because we'll answer the question "Where do you stand financially?" relative to a host of indicators. It also offers a few essential practices for anyone hoping to develop long-term financial stability.

If you don't care about why, consider going directly to chapter 19, "The Top 10: Your Next Dollar's Home," and get to work!

Tenet #3: Simple, not simplistic

Even that which I've deemed the Minimum Effective Dose of personal finance might feel overwhelming at times, especially if the subject matter is new to you. I'm sure there will be times when you'll think, "Uh, this doesn't exactly sound simple to me." Please take heart. It's part of the plan.

If I just give you a few bulleted action items with no background education or explanation, that would be overly simplistic, a cheapening of the advice, and ultimately detrimental to your long-term financial health. To get to elegant simplicity, we often have to wade through complexity.

Consider this quote attributed to Oliver Wendell Holmes Sr.: "For the simplicity on this side of complexity, I wouldn't give you a fig. But for the simplicity on the other side of complexity, for that I would give you anything I have."

An illustration of this principle: A Major League Baseball catcher flashes the pitcher a simple hand gesture, his recommendation for the next pitch. Once a pitcher has reached that level, he needn't retrace an elaborate mental framework to orchestrate a curveball, sinker, or fastball. But this process is only simple and efficient in the present because of the years of training and practice and the catcher's intimate knowledge of the pitcher's—as well as the batter's—strengths and weaknesses. The process is made simple thanks to the participants' willingness to endure the complex.

I strive to give you the simplicity on the *other* side of complexity. I reach for simple recommendations that are based on a deep and wide understanding of the complexity of these topics. And sometimes, I'll need to walk you through a helping of that complexity to ensure you can fully realize the benefits of these recommendations.

The Simplicity on the *Other* Side of Complexity

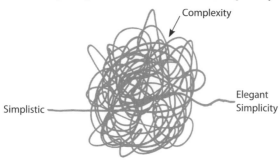

Parts 3 and 4 of the book—"Planning for the Inevitable" and "Planning for the Unexpected"—delve into the meat of personal finance and tap into the heart of its complexity. But don't worry, at the end of each chapter, you'll find a Simple Money Summary with concise, manageable guidance to help you accomplish the most with the least.

We conclude with part 5, "Planning for Action," because the best-laid plans are worthless if they are never implemented.

How to Use This Book

This book endeavors to provide a comprehensive overview of personal finance. It certainly won't touch on everything. For example, instead of a chapter on taxes, I discuss taxes throughout when appropriate. But the comprehensive scope means some sections will be more applicable than others to you.

Therefore, here's how I recommend approaching this book:

Part 1 is required reading. It's the foundation on which everything else is based. Even though you see very few references to money, if you were going to read only one section of the book, I'd implore you to read part 1.

Part 2 will be beneficial for everyone, but especially for those who wonder where they stand financially, those who are fearful they are behind, and those who are predisposed to saying, "Yeah, I'm really just not good with money."

Once you get to parts 3 and 4, if your attention is prone to wander or you have areas of special interest, you shouldn't be lost by going out of order. Take a glance at the chapter headings for your topics of choice.

To make the most of this book, I recommend keeping a Simple Money Journal. This is for two reasons:

1. The visual exercise of writing things down increases the impact of what you've learned.

2. As David Allen teaches us in his Getting Things Done (GTD) methodology, having a receptacle for things we want to remember declutters our brain space and thereby reduces our stress.

Throughout the book, you'll find Simple Money Journal Entry invitations where you can reflect on important questions, and at the end of each chapter I'll ask you to jot down any *insights* that strike you and the *actions* you choose to take as a result. Use your journal of choice—mine is the classic Moleskine—or use the Simple Money Journal that I've pre-populated with exercises and questions from each chapter (found at www.simplemoney.net/journal).

Part 5 is short but punchy, helping you apply whatever it is that you've learned for maximum effect. It functions best if you have used the "Insights and Actions" sections at the close of each chapter.

Tenet #4: Enough is "Enough"

It is, as the old Shaker song lyrics say, a gift to be simple, but simplicity is not an end in itself. It's the vehicle to something much more meaningful, and something very difficult to find in a financial landscape dominated by information overload and the emotions of fear and greed.

That is the place of Enough, and that's where we begin.

PART 1

PLANNING FOR LIFE

*Personal finance is more
personal than it is finance.*

1

ENOUGH

Redeeming Wealth

WHY do I need to read this chapter?

"How much money is enough?"

When asked this question, the richest American at the time, John D. Rockefeller Sr., responded, "Just a little bit more."

"More" is a disease that infects regardless of the level of our assets. If we put Rockefeller's quote within the context of his life and other quotes, it doesn't appear that it was a lust for money he hoped to satisfy, nor a quest for material security he hoped to gain, through his wealth building. Indeed, he also said, "I know of nothing more despicable and pathetic than a man who devotes all the hours of the waking day to the making of money for money's sake."[1]

So, it wasn't just about the money for him. Perhaps the real problem with Rockefeller's relationship to money lay in this interesting quote, a belief of his corroborated by other similar Rockefeller ruminations: "I believe it is a religious duty to get all the money you can, fairly and honestly; to keep all you can, and to give away all you can."[2]

For Rockefeller, the accumulation of money was a duty—a divine command, no less! Therefore, despite his affinity for acquisition, his thirst for more was, sadly, unquenchable. Even becoming the richest man in the world—perhaps in history[3]—was not Enough.

If you picked up this book hoping that it will help you make, save, invest, and accumulate a surplus of money, you'll likely find enough material to satisfy that aspiration. But if that is all you learn—how to acquire more—I will have failed. Then, this will be just another financial book that ultimately misses the mark.

While I do hope the lessons herein improve your balance sheet, I personally will be satisfied only if these pages lead you not merely to riches, but to a richer life. Not only to a cleaner balance sheet, but to a freer mind.

Yes, I want you to be debt free, financially independent, properly insured, and prepared for whatever life brings. But more than anything, I want you to live in the sweet satisfaction of Enough. The bad news, as we see with Rockefeller, is that money can't buy contentment. The good—I mean, great—news is that you can have Enough regardless of your circumstances.

You can be content now, and that's why you need to read this chapter. If you're anything like me, it's also why this will be the chapter you need to revisit periodically. After all, our tendency is to move away from Enough—not toward it.

The American Dream?

Tim Meeks is a mid-to-upper-level business director. He, his wife, Joy, and their children represent the prototypical middle-class American family on the cover of *Kiplinger's Personal Finance* magazine. But there's more to their story.

In the early 2000s, when homeownership seemed to be the smartest financial move to make, Tim got a touch of real-estate fever. He successfully parlayed his hunger for more into a small home-flipping and rental property business, doubling his net worth in one year and validating his dream of retirement as a thirtysomething.

Then the market turned. Violently. In a matter of months, hundreds of thousands of dollars of his family's real estate riches had vanished, along with everything else his family had ever saved—unbeknownst to Joy. Tim admitted to his wife that they had over a million dollars of unsupportable debt. They both had to claim personal bankruptcy.

Disgrace. Failure. Their darkest hours.

Today they rank that experience among the most important of their lives. They now define wealth not by how much they have in assets but how little they have in debt. Since the bankruptcy, they rented an affordable home, paid off all surviving loans, and repaired their credit sufficiently to buy a new home, five years to the month after claiming bankruptcy. The peace they found through hitting bottom has entirely changed their view of what really is Enough.

Enough is a relative term, but Pete, aka Mr. Money Mustache, has taken it to the next level. A capitalist and investor, he has rewritten the modern-day version of the middle-class American Dream. Pete decided he wasn't satisfied saving the requisite 10 percent of his income in his 401(k). Even 20 percent was too little. An engineer by trade, he crunched the numbers: If he could save 50 percent of his income starting at age 20, he could retire by age 37. If he could save 75 percent, his full-time career would be a measly 7 years. With little deviation from that path, and just in time for the birth of their first son, Mr. and now Mrs. Money Mustache retired, not into extravagance, but into Enough. At the age of thirty.

Truett Cathy, on the other hand, personified the American Dream. He was the billionaire Chick-fil-A restaurateur. Until his death in September 2014, this Depression survivor bristled if you referred to him as being rich. When asked if he thought wealth was worth all of its trappings and temptations, he replied flatly, "No."

"Wealth is only worth it if you find a way to freely and abundantly give." And give and give and give, if you look at his track record. He worked his fingers to the bone for the first half of his career and spent much of the remainder—still visiting the office into his nineties—finding ways to use his wealth and influence to better the lives of those less fortunate. He believed our wealth is measured by our contributions, not our withdrawals.

Few have made more dedicated contributions to the world's betterment than Anne and Stephanie Reynolds, a mother-daughter duo who, when vacationing in the Dominican Republic, accidentally wandered into Haiti, the poorest country in the Western Hemisphere. They landed in a tiny village without a school or modern amenities. They later dedicated themselves to the restoration of that village—but not because of what the people lacked. Instead, it is the wealth within the Haitian people that inspired the Reynolds women to make lifelong commitments in partnership.

Who could be more removed from the woes of the world's poorest inhabitants than American rock stars, scooting around in private jets, spending $10,000 on dinner and Dom for their entourage. Not Scott Avett from the Grammy-nominated punk-country band, The Avett Brothers. No prima donnas on their tour bus, and no love lost for the frenzy of fame and fortune, as evidenced in their song, "Ill with Want." Avett labors for a life far humbler than the rock star standard.

As for professional athletes, their earning power sadly seems to be eclipsed only by their penchant for parting with the money they earn. Severe financial distress—even bankruptcy—is an epidemic. Former NFL All-Pro defensive lineman Joe Ehrmann tasted the excessive lifestyle of professional sports in all of its facets until tragedy changed his trajectory. Profiled for his unorthodox yet highly successful coaching techniques in Jeffrey Marx's bestselling *Season of Life*, Joe educates professional and collegiate athletes and their coaches on building men and women not for themselves, but for others.

The original ideal of the American Dream—the promise of a land of opportunity—seems to have disintegrated into Dream 2.0, where opportunity is synonymous with money, riches, and wealth. And to our detriment, one of those words has been hijacked.

Redeeming Wealth

Words are important, even powerful. A well-placed word can lift us up or crush our spirit. The meaning of words can also shift over time, depending on who says them and how they're used. The words *money*, *riches*, and *wealth* offer a fascinating study in etymology for terms that now appear almost synonymous. *Money* and *riches* have always meant something very close to what they mean today—currency and an abundance thereof.

The word *wealth*, however, has a deeper and more powerful meaning, one that has been obscured through successful attempts to commercialize and sell the dream that abundant riches equate to a life without care. Wealth's true meaning is very close to the English words signifying contentment and Enough.

How is it that some people possess riches beyond even their most outlandish dreams, yet find contentment elusive?

How is it that others have nothing more than bare necessities, but rest easy with no fear of tomorrow?

Why do some billionaires share while others horde?

Why do some of our poorest neighbors recoil into bitter envy while others rise above seemingly impossible circumstances?

While it certainly is true that billions of the earth's inhabitants require more materially, even for mere survival, *we all need more Enough.*

How do you define true wealth—Enough? How do you define success? Please consider these five questions, shared courtesy of Carol Anderson, a personal finance researcher and founder of Money Quotient, a nonprofit devoted to a life-centered approach to financial planning.

Simple Money Journal Entry

Defining True Wealth

1. How do you define success in your working life?
2. How do you define success in your family (or home) life?
3. How do you define success in your financial life?
4. What do you need to be content?
5. How do you hope to be remembered someday?

Money Scripts

Before we can take the right actions in our personal finances, we must be sure to apply right thinking. This is because financial thoughts—or as the psychology of money gurus Rick Kahler and Ted Klontz call them, "Money Scripts"—precede and drive our actions. They are our underlying beliefs about money, the "beliefs behind the behaviors," as Kahler says.

To explain, Kahler reminded me of Daniel Kahneman's book, *Thinking, Fast and Slow*, in which Kahneman segregates the human brain into two systems:

System one is fast, automatic, frequent, stereotypic, and subconscious. It's the emotional brain. System two, on the other hand, is slow, effortful, logical, calculating, and conscious. It's the thinking or rational brain.[4]

Interestingly, 90 percent of our decisions—including financial decisions—are made in our emotional brain. It is in this part of our brain where Money Scripts are learned. Most of this prewiring takes place before the age of ten.

Money Scripts aren't necessarily true or false, right or wrong. They just are.

I often conduct an exercise in educational sessions that I lead. The audiences vary but are always relatively homogenous groups. Forty accounting students. Thirty theater performers and staff. Twenty-five clients of a financial advisory firm. Two hundred financial advisors. And what shocks me (and them) is how wide-ranging their responses are in this exercise.

The wealthy got that way by . . . everything from "working hard" and "investing well" to "inheritance" or even "taking advantage of people."

Poor people are poor because of . . . "a lack of education" or "bad circumstances" and, invariably, "they're lazy."

How is it that a group of people so similar to each other could have such disparate answers to the same questions? Regardless of how similar they appear now, they each had different parents, different childhoods, different friends, different educations, and most importantly, different reactions to each of these stimuli.

We've each had a different life.

For better and worse, our financial actions are entirely logical when our financial worldview comes into focus.

So what if we don't like what we see? How do we change it?

First, we acknowledge our current money beliefs and the experiences that led us to them. Then, we modify and rewrite a new script.

Is Money Good or Bad?

Here are the top ten Money Scripts, according to Kahler and Klontz:

- "Money is good."
- "Money is bad."
- "I don't deserve money."
- "I deserve to spend money."
- "There will never be enough money."
- "There will always be enough money."

- "Money is unimportant."
- "Money will give my life meaning."
- "It's not nice (or necessary) to talk about money."
- "If I'm good, the universe will supply all my material needs."[5]

Simple Money Journal Entry

Do you recognize any of your Money Scripts?

"Money is bad" breeds a bunch of new, dangerous baby scripts. "People who have money are bad" is easily followed by "Therefore, I will not have money."

I've had the privilege to counsel an executive of an international aid organization. In short, his job is to go to the most deprived places in the world and organize the relief necessary to raise the status of a community from critical to stable. His wife summarized his modus operandi, "Tyler has literally given someone the shirt off of his back—multiple times."

We met, in part, because Tyler had received an unexpected lump sum of money. It wasn't enough to become a full-time philanthropist, but it was a life-changing amount that could help to backfill the compounded savings deficit resulting from his persistently underpaid profession of career Samaritan.

At one point during our discovery session, I asked Tyler, "Having lived life in pursuit of helping those with *nothing*, can you handle having *something*? Or are you capable of committing financial suicide, of divesting yourself of these funds to salve your conscience?"

Tyler had to acknowledge that he was, indeed, capable of relinquishing his windfall and, therefore, his family's financial future. For him, *Enough* was *too much*. We had to rewrite the script.

I find that "Money is good" is even more pervasive and damaging, because it morphs quickly into "If money is good, more money is better," and finally devolves into "If I only had more money, I'd have a better life."

Sadly, this script never seems to lose its potency no matter how many times it is disproven. For example, *Sports Illustrated* found (and ESPN corroborated) that "by the time they have been retired for two years, 78% of former NFL players have gone bankrupt or are under financial stress" and "within five years of retirement, an estimated 60% of former NBA players are broke."[6]

Rock stars, actors and actresses, lottery winners? The numbers are all similar. The National Endowment for Financial Education estimates that 70 percent of people who suddenly receive life-changing money are separated from it within three years.[7]

Indeed, "change" seems to be the operative word, according to Susan Bradley, founder of the Sudden Money Institute and author of *Sudden Money: Managing a Financial Windfall.*[8] "When life changes, money changes—and when money changes, life changes," says Bradley.[9]

Even when the money is well-managed, the "more money, more better" script is still a killer. When we believe that money is inherently good, it often puts us at odds with the people we claim to prioritize over money—family and friends. Deeming money "good" personifies it, and the people in our lives simply can't compete with our relationship with an inanimate object that silently promises to make all of our dreams come true.

The truth is that we don't—or perhaps shouldn't—have a relationship with money. That gives it too much credit.

Money is neither good nor bad. It's a neutral tool that can be used well or poorly, for good or ill.

Those who think money is inherently bad tend to manage it poorly, straining relationships. Those who "love money" and think it is inherently good tend to strain relationships, deprioritizing the people in their lives. And, by the way, straining relationships also tends to cost money—half of your money, typically.

Meanwhile, those who view money as a neutral tool tend to employ and attract it most effectively.

Rewriting the Script

So I asked Rick Kahler, the Money Script guy, "How can we rewrite Money Scripts?" The answer, Kahler said, comes in the form of four questions patterned after Byron Katie's work in her book, *Loving What Is:*[10]

Simple Money Journal Entry

Rewriting Money Scripts

1. Is the Money Script true?
2. Can you *absolutely* know it is true?
3. What happens when you believe the Money Script? (Who are you when you think that? How do you react?)
4. What or who would you be without the Money Script?

Now, modify and rewrite your Money Script.

One of the most powerful tools in rewriting the script comes, I've found, in seeking out new experiences.

Hope in Hell on Earth

For months I had prepared myself for a particular moment, stepping off of the run-down school bus in the middle of La Chureca, the dump of Nicaragua's capital city, Managua. Listed among the Seven Horrendous Wonders of the World, La Chureca is not just a collection of refuse, but also a refuge for more than three hundred families.[11] Men, women, and children compete with mangy dogs for sustenance and sex traffickers for their minds, bodies, and souls.

I knew it was coming from the moment I accepted the invitation to join a contingent of teachers and health and finance professionals orchestrated by GraceCity, a young church in downtown Baltimore enamored with serving the poorest of the poor in its hometown and, interestingly, the Managua city dump. But nothing could prepare me for the sights: homes manufactured of rubbish; smoke lifting from piles of debris; a multicolored landscape of mountainous trash dotted with laborers scrounging for something of worth under a 98-degree sun; a makeshift school lined with barbed wire;[12] and scores of children, many without shoes or a single article of clean clothing but with stunning smiles lighting up their dirty faces. After all, they were thrilled to see us—we were there with the ORPHANetwork, a Virginia-based non-governmental organization (NGO) devoted to serving malnourished and displaced children in Nicaragua. We were at one of their many feeding centers in the country, designed to provide at least one nutritious meal per day to more than 10,000 starving children.

You hear of such things on the news and see pictures of such children on commercials filled with brown faces asking for money on late-night television, but it's hard to believe it's true—that I was fortunate enough to be born in a geographic location with a host of inherent benefits while these kids were born into the closest thing imaginable to hell on Earth. When I gaze into my own children's eyes, I see in them a vast universe of unencumbered curiosity and possibility, but in La Chureca, I was forced to look into the eyes of girls as young as six who have already been sold into prostitution.

It was as if I was in one of those movies when a scene strikes a subject so hard that all he can do is marvel in slow motion, unable to process the myriad of overwhelming stimuli. But as my worldview crumbled and my eyes welled up with tears, I was forced to turn my gape downward. A young boy was tugging on my shorts. Once our eyes met, he thrust his hands upward in the universal sign for "Pick me up," and before I could confirm that I'd been vaccinated for all that he was visibly carrying, he'd swung himself up onto my back, stripped my sunglasses and made them his own, smacked my side, and yelled "Vamos!" Just a kid. Any kid. Born in a garbage dump.

This experience rewrote a number of my personal Money Scripts and will no doubt continue to do so. This interaction with people who genuinely suffered from a dire lack of enough changed my definition of Enough.

This moment changed my entire worldview. It altered my values and priorities, which are the foundation of every successful financial plan—and the topic of our next chapter.

Simple Money "Enough" Summary

1. The original meaning of the word *wealth* is actually contentment—Enough. We all need more Enough, and each chapter of this book will be oriented around this concept.

2. Our predisposition to dealing with money is formed through our life experiences, especially those in the first ten years of life. These underlying beliefs are Money Scripts that often dictate our behavior, whether or not we know it.

3. Money Scripts that we don't like can be rewritten through self-analysis and new experiences.

What INSIGHTS and ACTIONS did you take from this chapter?

2

VALUES

Three Questions to Guide You

WHY do I need to read this chapter?

The whole notion of values is a touchy subject because it's so hard to grasp. What exactly *are* values?

The term means different things to different people. To some, values are the pillars of existence, while others view them as a collection of subjective mores used by the former group to judge everyone else. But if we strip this concept of its rhetorical baggage, I believe we do find something of great, uh, value.

Our values are simply the stuff in life that we want to be about. That which we want to define us. The guideposts we choose to live by.

They are the priorities that we hope will mark our time on this earth. They are the elements of life that motivate us; that when satisfied, bring us genuine contentment. Enough.

They are neither universal nor constant. Our values may, indeed, change as we change, but they are also not fleeting.

Values are critical in financial planning as anchors for our goals and boundaries for the actions we take to achieve them. But most of all, they make the hardest decisions in life much easier by helping us prioritize what truly is the most important.

Understanding what you value most will help simplify even the most complex financial decisions.

Virtue and Vice

Perhaps the most famous articulation of one's values belongs to founding father Benjamin Franklin. At the age of twenty, Franklin created a system to help shape his character. Indeed, Franklin described the purpose of his system, based on a list of his "Thirteen Virtues," and his attempted application of it in his autobiography.

He lists a single word followed by a clarifying sentence. Here is a sample:

1. *Temperance*: Eat not to dullness; drink not to elevation. . . .
4. *Resolution*: Resolve to perform what you ought; perform without fail what you resolve. . . .
7. *Sincerity*: Use no hurtful deceit; think innocently and justly, and, if you speak, speak accordingly. . . .
11. *Tranquility*: Be not disturbed at trifles, or at accidents common or unavoidable.[1]

While Franklin's virtues have been used as the foundation of many values-oriented habit generation systems—most notably international leadership authority Stephen Covey's—I believe we benefit more from seeing how Franklin failed than how he succeeded. In conceiving the Thirteen Virtues, Old Ben dedicated himself to, in his own words, "the bold and arduous project of arriving at moral perfection. I wish'd to live without committing any fault at any time; I would conquer all that either natural inclination, custom, or company might lead me into."[2]

The result? "I was surpris'd to find myself so much fuller of faults than I had imagined," Franklin confesses.[3]

Has this been far from your experience, when attempting to conform to any personal or financial ideal? It certainly has been mine, and I believe it is the top reason that so few resolutions are indeed performed "without fail." How frustrating it is to see our efforts toward self-improvement more expedient at revealing our vices than our virtues.

Therefore, any effort to establish a set of ideals—virtues or values—to which we align ourselves and our money must be accompanied by an allowance for imperfection, which *is* both universal and constant. Then, like Franklin, instead of abandoning our resolve to eliminate our faults, we might at least "enjoy the satisfaction of seeing them diminish."

"I can't get no . . ."

Yes, satisfaction is what we're after, because satisfaction leads to contentment and toward the elusive Enough. So let's conduct a quick experiment in satisfaction. The objective is to gauge your level of satisfaction in several areas of life—not just the financial realm. This is beneficial for many reasons, but especially because money touches nearly every facet of life, like it or not.

Simple Money Journal Entry

Wheel of Life

The Wheel of Life instructions are, dare I say, simple. You rate your satisfaction in each area of life between 0 and 10. Zero is the worst, represented as the center of the wheel, and 10 is the best, at the end of each spoke. After you plot your satisfaction for each facet of life, then connect the dots to behold the size and shape of your wheel. Go ahead, give it a whirl!

The Wheel of Life

The Wheel of Life has many applications, but the primary aim of this exercise in self-awareness is to "put money in the context of life," according to Carol Anderson of Money Quotient.

It's almost impossible to complete this exercise, as I regularly do, without generating some lightbulb moments. "Ooh, interesting . . ." "Ahh, disappointing . . ."

But the exercise goes beyond mere contemplation and begins to unveil some of those things that we value most. Of course, there may be some spokes on the wheel where you feel quite satisfied, perhaps because they're important to you and your appreciation, therefore, shows in your performance.

Now consider those areas where you rated your satisfaction as subpar. Is it possible that you score yourself lowly in these areas because you actually value them a great deal? Perhaps these are important areas of life that are simply being overwhelmed by the tyranny of the urgent.

Franklin's Failure

Franklin failed to attain perfection in his behavior management system in part because of his inherent imperfection, but also because of misplaced motivation, which is a topic we'll explore in detail in the next chapter. He directly acknowledged as much: "My list of virtues contain'd at first but twelve; but a Quaker friend having kindly informed me that I was generally thought proud; . . . and I added Humility to my list," later lamenting, "I cannot boast of much success in acquiring the *reality* of this virtue."[4]

He couldn't even avoid using the word "boast" in admitting his inability to conquer pride! And while I would agree with Franklin that humility is an admirable trait to work toward regardless, it's quite possible that his virtuous success rate may have been higher if the values he listed were those he felt *im*pelled—not *com*pelled—to list.

How, then, should we discern our uniquely personal picture of values and ensure it remains untainted by those bent on compelling us into conformity? While some may be inclined to commit themselves, as Franklin did, to authoring a linear list of thirteen ideals followed by a tactical plan for accomplishing them through goals, others may be inclined to list only three, or none.

Or better yet, forget lists and collections altogether. I'm convinced that the most vociferous proponents of lists and goal setting are the analytically oriented who are predisposed to these methods. It may be more helpful, and no less effective, for you to communicate your values through a collage of pictures, a song, or a story.

Kinder's Three Questions

Consider George Kinder's method. Kinder is a Harvard-trained economist turned philosopher turned accountant turned spiritual-teacher whose work on the intersection of money and life is very well respected, even in the financial industry.

Kinder, elsewhere and in his book *The Seven Stages of Money Maturity*, introduced the world to a new way to explore our values, especially as related to our finances. It involves simply reflecting on three questions that dig into our deepest motivations. Please respond to each in order, ideally in writing, and then we'll reflect together.

Simple Money Journal Entry

Kinder's Three Questions

Question One: Imagine that you are financially secure, that you have enough money to take care of your needs, now and in the future. The question is,

How would you live your life?

What would you do with the money?

Would you change anything?

Let yourself go. Don't hold back your dreams. Describe a life that is complete, that is richly yours.

Question Two: This time, you visit your doctor, who tells you that you have five to ten years left to live. The good part is that you won't ever feel sick. The bad news is that you will have no notice of the moment of your death.

What will you do in the time you have remaining to live?

Will you change your life, and how will you do it?

Question Three: This time, your doctor shocks you with the news that you have only one day left to live. Notice what feelings arise as you confront your very real mortality. Ask yourself,

What dreams will be left unfulfilled?

What do I wish I had finished or who do I wish I
   had been?

What do I wish I had done?

What did I miss?

Now, let's consider the implications of each of these questions and how they're designed to draw valuable information from us. In Question One, Kinder first strips life of its financial stressors. But notice, this isn't the same as asking, "So, if you won the lottery, what would you do with the money?" He's asking what we would do with life if money was no issue. He tries to bring us to a hypothetical state of contentment when he says, "You are financially secure . . . you have enough . . . now and in the future." No surprise, eh, that we're back to the subject of *Enough*?

Then, before asking what we'd do with our money, Kinder invites us to explore how we would live our life. He gives us a moment to consider how we'd handle the money, but then we wade into much deeper waters—"Would you change anything?"

I find that the answers to Question One are often a rephrasing of what our most important goals are, a topic addressed in depth in the next chapter. But now, in Question Two, Kinder takes off the gloves.

Perhaps you tuned out as soon as you got into this question. Most people don't want to think about being put in this position. Maybe this struck too close to home because you or a loved one has endured the I've-got-some-bad-news discussion and its aftermath. If so, I encourage you to consider that these questions are far more about life than death.

The first time I read Question Two, I approached it too literally. Most people, I retorted internally, can't just decide (or afford) to live life as though they knew they were going to die within the next ten years! But then I realized that the point of this query is simply to evoke a better answer to the question, What are your most deeply held values? Many of us will start talking about family, relationships, and bucket-list items. Another purpose of Question Two is to prepare us for the third question.

If you really engage Question Three, you'll get beyond superficial answers and start to unveil what really drives and motivates you. Unlike the second question, where there might be some overlap between your answers and those of other people, the third question begins to elicit longings that are unique to you.

Simple Money Journal Entry

Your Life's Priorities

As you consider your answers to Kinder's questions and revisit your Wheel of Life, what comes through as that which you most value—your life's priorities?

Please consider that if you have too many, then nothing is a priority. I challenge you to keep the number of priorities small—no more than seven, maybe fewer.

If lists don't suit you, try writing a statement, sentence, or paragraph to express what is most important to you. And if you, like me, are a visual person, I encourage you to create a collage of pictures or drawings representing your primary motivators. Keep it in your home or office as a vibrant reminder. (See a great example from author and early Twitter hire, Claire Díaz-Ortiz, on her website.[5])

However you arrange your priorities, it is vital that they are prioritized. None of us can attain everything we desire in money and life in an instant. Both our financial and human capital are finite. We can't have it all, all at once.

Although prioritization might be the simplest tool in this book, it is actually the most powerful and perpetually useful, because most of the decisions we make in financial planning ultimately come down to effective prioritization. And it's satisfaction in the areas in life we deem most important that lead us to Enough.

Priorities take the guesswork out of difficult decisions and give us confidence in setting the goals we'll work toward, the subject of our next chapter.

Simple Money Values Summary

1. Understanding our priorities, or values, helps to guide our planning and make life's most complex decisions simpler.

2. Ben Franklin's "Thirteen Virtues" exercise for patterning his life after what he valued most teaches us a great deal. But we learn more from how (and why) Franklin failed than how he succeeded.

3. Your completion of the Wheel of Life and your answers to George Kinder's Three Questions are incredibly effective tools in determining the aim of this chapter—spelling out your true priorities in life.

What INSIGHTS and ACTIONS
did you take from this chapter?

3

RIDING THE ELEPHANT

Unconventional Goal Setting

WHY do I need to read this chapter?

Goals. Do you have a positive or negative impression of that word? For some, goals are highly motivating, but for many others, the word *goals* sounds like chores.

Whatever your predisposition, I invite you to consider goals simply as the natural outgrowth of our priorities in life, our values (chap. 2). Once we've declared what we want to be about, goals take us beyond philosophy to application.

Goals are our values in motion, advancing our dreams from ideation to action so we and those we serve can benefit from them. Goals are the mileposts on the road to Enough.

Carrots and Sticks

Wrestling with his success and failure in achieving human perfection in the early 1700s, Benjamin Franklin may well have been exhibiting behavior that the science of motivation wouldn't discover for more than two hundred years. Between 1949 and 1969, psychologist Harry Harlow discovered and psychology professor Edward Deci confirmed that "carrots and sticks"—rewards for good behavior and punishments for bad—weren't the best way to motivate people (or even primates).

So why is the carrot and the stick still the primary way we work, manage, parent, and even discipline ourselves in order to perform that long list of tasks we know we *should* do?

As Daniel Pink articulates so well in his book *Drive*, "Too many . . . still operate from assumptions about human potential and individual performance that are outdated, unexamined, and rooted more in folklore than science."[1]

Instead, Pink suggests that the best motivators come from within, not without:

1. *Autonomy*—the desire to direct our own lives
2. *Mastery*—the urge to make progress and get better at something that matters
3. *Purpose*—the yearning to do what we do in the service of something larger than ourselves[2]

As it turns out, "you *can*" is actually a better motivator than "you *should*."

"Should-Mongering"

Sadly, no one is better at "should" than the financial establishment:

"You *should* be making more on your CD!"

"You *should* be earning more in your investments!"

"You *should* be better protecting your family from destitution with our life insurance!"

This fatal motivational flaw is not isolated to banks, brokerage firms, and insurance companies either. Here are a few direct quotes from some of the biggest names in financial self-help:

> "You *should* have at least an eight-month emergency fund saved up."
>
> "You *should* never buy a new car unless you have a net worth of a million dollars."
>
> "You *should* never buy without waiting overnight."

I'm not suggesting that any of these "shoulds" are inherently wrong (or right), but the rampant should-mongering in the financial landscape has simply not worked.

It hasn't worked for the same reasons that more than 80 percent of the recommendations made by financial advisors are not implemented by those who sought the advice. It hasn't worked for the same reasons that SMART goals aren't effective for so many well-intended goal-setters.

The Problems with SMART Goals

The SMART goal-setting system requires that a goal must be *Specific*, *Measurable*, *Attainable*, *Realistic*, and *Tangible* to be valid. I have both subscribed to this regime and taught a similar version of it. The SMART system is the goal-setting standard, the rarely questioned convention.

But.

Despite its acronymic ring, it misses the mark.

Why? In short, it is unnecessarily restrictive. It limits our imagination, constricts our potential, and drains our inspiration.

Do you remember our brain dissection in chapter 1, differentiating between the rational, logical *thinking* brain and the instinctive, subconscious *emotional* brain? The emotional brain makes 90 percent of our decisions. Meanwhile, SMART goals are speaking *only* to our thinking brain, ignoring the emotional brain that's so often driving the ship. SMART goals might tell us *what* to do and *how* to do it, but they scarcely address *why* and therefore don't effectively motivate us to action. This is why New Year's resolutions routinely fail and financial planning recommendations are not implemented. We're talking to the wrong brain.

Jonathan Haidt, the author of *The Happiness Hypothesis* and professor at New York University Stern School of Business, has no such problem. He talks to both the Elephant and its Rider:

> The mind is divided in many ways, but the division that really matters is between conscious/reasoned processes and automatic/implicit processes. These two parts are like a rider on the back of an elephant. The rider's inability to control the elephant by force explains many puzzles about our mental life, particularly why we have such trouble with weakness of will. Learning how to train the elephant is the secret of self-improvement.[3]

Sound familiar? Yes, these two parts of the brain that Haidt describes as the Elephant and Rider are the same to which Kahler and Kahneman referred in chapter 1 as system one and system two. In Haidt's example, the Elephant is the emotional brain (system one) and its Rider, the thinking brain (system two).

Why an elephant and not a horse—or donkey? Because this isn't a political argument, it's physiological. The emotional brain's analogous size advantage over the Rider requires an animal as large as an elephant.

SMART goals assume that the Rider, the master, is the only party that matters, but Chip and Dan Heath dispute this in their book *Switch: How to Change Things When Change Is Hard*. They think the Elephant gets a bad rap. They write: "But what may surprise you is that the Elephant also has enormous strengths and that the Rider has crippling weaknesses."[4]

"To make progress toward a goal," the Heath brothers suggest, "requires the energy and drive of the Elephant. If you want to change things, you've got to appeal to both."[5]

You've got to appeal to your Elephant.

Unconventional Goals

How, then, can we appeal to both the emotional and thinking brain—the Elephant and the Rider—in the context of goal setting and financial planning?

We begin by appealing to the motivational muscle in our duo, the emotional Elephant in the room, borrowing from Daniel Pink's logic in *Drive*:

First, our goals must be autonomous—*self-selected*. We're more likely to stay the course when we're impelled from within rather than compelled by an outside force. This is not to suggest that willingly submitting ourselves to the accountability of an outside force is not beneficial. Doing so may even be an essential ingredient to successfully achieving our goals, but the decision to do so must be ours.

Next, our goals must be *authentic*—authentically ours—consistent with our individual gifts and proclivities. It must be something that we are capable of mastering. Successories motivational posters might want you to believe that you can achieve anything that your heart desires, but it's simply not true.

I am five feet seven (and one-half) inches tall. I weigh 137 pounds (soaking wet). I have a modicum of athletic ability, but I've never been picked first when teams are made. Regardless of how much I may have wanted to believe that I could be a middle linebacker in the National Football League, regardless of how much I may have practiced, it was never going to happen. I was simply not endowed with the body or innate skill required to compete athletically at that level in that sport.

I am all for "reach" goals—even Jim Collins's "Big Hairy Audacious Goals"—but we must have the baseline ability to master the tasks necessary to achieve the goal.

When we begin to master an activity that is self-selected, the Elephant and Rider begin to work surprisingly well together. The Elephant is satisfied because it's doing what it wants to do, while the Rider is able to appreciate the positive outcome. The Rider begins to channel the Elephant's brawn to even greater effect, creating a circular cycle of proficiency. Everybody's happy.

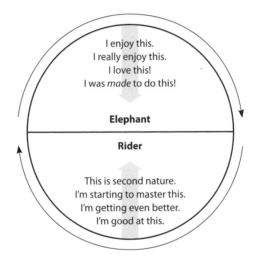

Lastly, our newfound success really blossoms into satisfaction when we are driven by a purpose bigger than us, individually; when we are *others-oriented*. I could spend several paragraphs justifying this third-goal criterion with statistics and studies, but there's no need—because you already know this, don't you? We already know that we're wired to do something meaningful with others, for others.

We already know that some of life's greatest satisfaction comes from helping satisfy the needs of others.

Profit as Purpose?

You may not be aware that in the corporate realm there is an ideology insisting that profit *is* purpose. That a corporation can do no greater good for itself, its shareholders, and society than to profit, which presumably will create jobs, stimulate the economy, and build wealth.

This is precisely the willful, intellectual blindness that led to the financial crises of the late 2000s.

This is hogwash.

Profit is a good thing, but profit is not purpose. It's purpose fuel.

There are also immense pragmatic benefits to expending our effort with and on behalf of others. First, affirmation from other collaborators on and beneficiaries of our work energizes the Elephant and boosts its endurance. And second, the skilled Rider solicits and receives constructive criticism, further refining the pair's output.

As the circular collaboration between the Rider and the Elephant generates momentum for the self-selected goal, the others-centered orientation begins to add mass that builds and builds into a success snowball.

At this stage, we must not restrict our goal construction to the domain of dollars and cents. It may even be helpful to strip our goals of their direct financial implications to begin with.

The Danger Zone

We didn't want to stifle the creativity of our emotional brain at the onset of this chapter with the rigidity of SMART criteria. We needed the freedom of autonomy to tap into our drive mechanism—our source of motivation—supported by our unique giftedness.

Now we can borrow some SMART characteristics to crystalize our values and priorities into actual goals. But be warned, this is a dangerous step. Fear sets in and threatens to bring a halt to the goal-setting process for two reasons:

1. We fear that we'll fail.
2. We fear that we'll succeed.

By specifying a goal, and especially by establishing a timeline, we generate a measuring stick that we might not live up to. We might just be setting ourselves up for failure. And fail we may. Indeed,

you

will

fail.

Once you acknowledge that failure is a necessary by-product of goal setting, the fear of failure begins to lose its power. If your goal is self-selected, authentically yours, and others-oriented, failure actually becomes your guide. It helps inform your process and refine your strategy.

But just as powerful, if not more so, is the fear of success. How could this be true when the entire aim of goal setting is to engineer success? It can be summed up in one word:

Change

In order to achieve any goal, change is required. Then, if you achieve your goal, it's altogether likely that your success will birth new changes. Consider the change required in the case of this single, unrefined goal: "Find my dream job."

First, you'll have to expend time and money to identify the job and then gain the education necessary to develop new skill sets. Then, you may have the pleasure of disappointing your current employer and co-workers when you deliver the news.

And that's all before the big change—starting a new job and often taking a pay cut. Letting the family know that cell phone plans and cable television need to be trimmed. You might have to move, even downsize.

In most cases, the changes required to see goals through are sacrifices. Often they are sacrifices borne by folks other than you. The reward doesn't come until after the sacrifice, and sometimes no externally apparent reward ever comes. But that is the worthy price of following your dreams.

Adventure

In 2013, my wife and I gave ourselves permission to consider a goal we'd previously deemed unthinkable—to pick up our family of four, leave a lifetime of family and friends in our beloved Baltimore, and move to a place where we knew no one—in search of a lower cost of living, a higher standard of living, and a more deliberate pace of life. We were going to go on an adventure.

Like many, this goal immediately turned into a project, a series of smaller goals, and actions to be taken:

- Research potential new areas, communities, schools, neighborhoods, churches.
- Determine feasibility of a satellite location with work.
- Leak our intentions to family.
- Schedule due diligence visits.
- Seek wise counsel.
- Decide.
- Announce plans to family and friends.
- Arrange move.
- And the hardest of all, leave our home, family, and friends.

It wasn't until June of 2014 that we moved to Charleston, South Carolina, and the adventure has really just begun.

Pursuing goals is dangerous business. This is why most are content to live within the safe confines of statements that begin with the two words, "I wish." But adventures begin with a simple yet challenging "I will."

"I will _____."

It is with these two words that hopes and dreams evolve into reality—goals and plans. It's entirely likely that you've begun to develop some goals as you've completed the exercises in this and previous chapters, but now it's time to complete process and refine your goals.

The first three points get the Elephant on board, but now it's time to let the Rider do his work. The Rider is much more amenable to the SMART process and borrows from it heavily.

Unconventional Goal Setting

Ensure that goals are . . .

1. *Self-selected*—yours, not someone else's.
2. *Authentic*—consistent with your personal gifting and attributes.
3. *Others-oriented*—a cause that is bigger than you alone.

Now you're ready to . . .

4. *Articulate* your goals, with as much specificity as possible.
5. *Test* your goals for attainability.
6. *Confirm* that the actions required don't conflict with values or priorities.
7. *Schedule* next actions and/or *establish* habits.

By articulating your goal, you slay your fear of failure, success, and change. It can truly be a cathartic experience, whether verbally or in writing. As you affix your statement with a period at the end, you're able to breathe deeply and acknowledge, "Well, that wasn't so bad, was it?"

Specificity is your friend here, but we also must acknowledge that some goals lend themselves to specificity and measurability (and tangibility) more than others. Many goals grow in clarity as we progress in this process, so refine along the way.

Lastly, all of this ideation amounts to little unless it is realized in the form of action. If your goal is to make a peanut butter, jelly, and banana sandwich, the chances are good that you'll be able to lay out a sequence of steps to achieve it. But for many of life's goals, future actions may be dictated, or at least informed, by the results of previous actions.

This is where I find productivity guru David Allen's Getting Things Done (GTD) methodology especially helpful. In GTD terminology, a goal is likely a "project." Many "actions," or tasks, are required to complete it. While most productivity systems compel you to adopt a detailed ranking system—think A, B, Cs and 1, 2, 3s—Allen finds that effort superfluous, if not counterproductive. He recommends simply glancing at the list of actions and deciding which one should be your "next action." This not only simplifies and streamlines the process, but it also gives you a regular infusion of Elephant-inspiring autonomy.

This is important because we are entirely capable of creating a system—even of our own volition—that ultimately becomes a force against which we, ourselves, will rebel. If the Rider gets too demanding, the Elephant may veer off course or collapse from exhaustion.

Show Me the Money

You may have noticed that we haven't touched on money much at all yet. That's because, as I mentioned in the introduction, *personal finance is a great deal more personal than it is finance.*

Most of our goals aren't financial goals anyway—they're life goals with financial implications. But if you'd like to see this unconventional process at work in the context of a conventional personal financial goal, here's a great example:

> "I want to retire" is a dream held by many, but it's not a goal yet. First, let's solicit the Elephant's motivational might. Why do you want to retire?

> "I've devoted the majority of my adult waking hours to a job that pays well but that I don't particularly enjoy. I'm not running from work, but I'd rather devote more of my time to my family, travel, and causes that I'm passionate about."

Self-selected—check. Authentic—check. Others-oriented—check. Okay, now we're getting somewhere. But we need to articulate the goal with more precision:

> "I want to retire comfortably in fifteen years," brings some much-needed specificity to this dream.

> "I want to retire in fifteen years and generate $75,000 per year without earned income," introduces some hard numbers that now allow us to measure our progress.

But here comes the moment of truth—the attainability test. Without knowing where you stand today, and what you will be able to save over the next fifteen years, there is no way to tell if your fledgling goal is attainable. For instance, if you were hoping to generate 100 percent of your income without the aid of a corporate pension or Social Security retirement benefit, you'd want approximately $1,875,000 in your retirement savings to reasonably anticipate generating $75,000 in income per year with any chance of outpacing inflation.

Therefore, if you're fifty years old and you already have $700,000 in savings, and the ability to save an additional $20,000 per year for the next fifteen years, your goal should pass the attainability test. That's assuming you're able to earn an average of at least 5 percent per year on your investments.

> "I want to retire in fifteen years and generate a minimum of $75,000 per year from my retirement savings, which should reach more than $2 million by earning an average 5 percent rate of return on my $700,000 nest egg plus an additional $20,000 of savings per year."

That works. That's a goal.

But what if saving $20,000 per year became a hardship? What if it would mean working substantially more, or picking up side jobs just as you'd committed to attending all of your daughter's college lacrosse games? In this case, the retirement *goal* may conflict with the *value* of being present for your family.

Goals should not compromise our values or rearrange our priorities.

If we don't hold to this standard, we are likely to suffer in one of at least two ways. Either we fall short on our goals because we lack the conviction or we allow our values to be compromised.

This final criterion is extremely helpful when making especially difficult decisions. We simply can't do it all—and we certainly can't do it all right now. Grounding our goals on the foundation of our values helps us discern what goals to go after and when, and what goals we can rule out.

Habits and Next Actions

Of course, your work has only just begun once you've established goals that meet the necessary criteria. How, then, do you move forward? It is through establishing habits and identifying "next actions."

First, let's recall the fully-formed goal:

"I want to retire in fifteen years and generate a minimum $75,000 per year from my retirement savings that should reach over $2 million by earning an average 5 percent rate of return on my $700,000 nest egg plus an additional $20,000 of savings per year."

The habit required to meet this goal is saving $20,000 per year. But where and how? That's where next actions come in. If you get a match to your 401(k) contributions at work, it's likely best to use that receptacle as your primary savings vehicle. If not, and depending on your tax bracket, it may make sense to use a combination of your 401(k) and your Roth IRA. (More on those in chap. 11 on retirement.)

Your actions, therefore, may be to do the following:

1. Increase the automatic monthly 401(k) contributions to 6 percent of salary.
2. Open a Roth IRA account.
3. Establish an automatic Roth contribution of $300 per month from checking account.

Your *next* action: "Go online to increase 401(k) contribution to 6 percent of salary."

"Next action" is a term made popular by GTD-guy David Allen, who differentiates between the majority of ambiguous to-do list items and optimal next actions: "The Next Action definition (if you're really getting down to having no ambiguity about the next visible physical activity required to move something forward), actually finishes the thinking you've implicitly agreed with yourself that you'll do."[6]

Therefore, the word *retirement* written down as a bullet on a legal pad is not a next action. Even "increase retirement savings" falls short. Allen pledges that we'll preserve more available space in our brains by putting as much information as is necessary in our stated to-dos. "Go online to increase 401(k) contribution to 6 percent of salary" should pass GTD scrutiny and ultimately save you time.

Here's what your goal might look like now on paper:

Goal Construction Exercise

Goal: _Retire in 15 years & generate a minimum $75,000/yr. from retirement savings that should reach over $2 million by earning an average 5% rate of return on $700,000 nest egg + additional $20,000 of savings per year._

Criteria:

How is it self-selected? _It is autonomy that I seek!_

Authentically mine? _Yes, I'm confident that I have much to offer outside of the workplace._

Others-oriented? _Yes, I look forward to reinvesting into my family, friends, and causes._

What actions need to be taken?

1) Increase 401k to 6%

2) Open a Roth IRA

3) Auto invest $300/mo in Roth

What is the next action? _Go online to increase 401k contribution to 6%_

Date completed: _____

> ### *Simple Money Journal Entry*
> Compound what you've learned in this chapter by
> writing out a fully articulated goal or two.

Thanks to the tangible nature of this retirement goal, you will be able to assess whether or not you're on track over the next fifteen years. The biggest challenge will be to navigate the temperamental nature of the financial markets.

This is not an uncommon phenomenon in goal setting and management, however. In many, if not most, examples, there are forces upon which our success is determinant. Some of these forces are within our control, others we have no power over. Our job is to control what we can and adjust to what we can't.

Of course, while we lack control over many elements of investing, we can exert control over some, a task that we tackle in depth in chapter 9 on investing.

But what do we do when a goal is especially lofty—seemingly out of reach, even?

1. Break it down into subgoals.
2. Generate next actions that are within our control.
3. Establish habits that can lead to future success.

Your Plan

This entire chapter—frankly, the entire book—is guidance, not ideology. My "system" is really a synthesis of thoughts designed to help you create your own plan. I am your advisor—you're the boss.

You are autonomous, the master of your own domain, and brimming with purpose, fully capable of creating goals that are self-selected, authentically yours, and designed to put your personal and financial resources to work serving others on the road to Enough.

Simple Money Goals Summary

1. Goals are our values in motion, unambiguous dreams. The SMART goal-setting system—suggesting goals should be specific, measurable, attainable, realistic, and tangible—is a valuable resource, but fundamentally flawed.

2. The carrot-and-stick motivational methodology has been proven *not* to work—but we're still using it. In his book *Drive*, Daniel Pink introduces us to a better way to motivate, through the tools of *autonomy*, *mastery*, and *purpose*. As it turns out, "you *can*" is a better motivator than "you *should*."

3. Our goals must appeal both to the Elephant and its Rider. The Elephant represents our emotional brain and is responsible for making 90 percent of our financial decisions. The Rider represents our rational, thinking brain. We need to enlist both of them in order to give us a chance to achieve our goals.

4. As we move from brainstorming about goals to actually creating them, two barriers rise before us: the fear of failure and, surprisingly, the fear of success. Fortunately, failure is a necessary by-product of goal setting. And it's not really success that we fear but the change it brings.

5. Unconventional goal setting satisfies the Elephant and then directs the Rider.

What INSIGHTS and ACTIONS did you take from this chapter?

4

CALLING

Finding Life-Giving Work

WHY do I need to read this chapter?

"I was *made* to do this." The moment when you see your innate gifts align with your passion for something—anything—it can send chills down your spine. Whether it's on the baseball field, in the classroom, at a drafting table, in the kitchen, behind the wheel, at a computer, in front of a crowd, or in the boardroom, the thrill is undeniable. Most people get glimpses of these moments, but for too many of us, it's merely a fleeting glance.

We need not rely on happenstance to enjoy these moments. Indeed, life can and should be lived in pursuit of them. There is, however, a method to this pursuit.

You've wrestled with Enough and examined your financial tendencies in chapter 1. You've explored your values and stated your priorities in chapter 2. You've created a framework for establishing goals in chapter 3. The synthesis of these three achievements—infused with the revelation that comes from benchmark life experiences—leads us to our calling. It may not necessarily be found in our work, but calling and career are an excellent marriage that often leads to personal fulfillment and financial prosperity.

Finding Your Calling

What is it that drives a person, even if it happens to be in pursuit of a goal with little probability of coming to fruition? For my brother, Jon, a musician, it's an easy decision. It's almost as if he doesn't have a choice. For him, music isn't just a job. It's part of who he is. It's a vocation—his calling. To anyone who sees him perform, this becomes obvious.

Like many artists, he never tires of the work. This is the foremost sign that you are living out your calling. My brother labors, often to the point of physical exhaustion. But his effort itself is rewarding and life-giving. Whether he's pounding out a new song in his basement, playing at a bar until 2:00 a.m., or performing for thousands under the spotlight, the labor is its own reward.

Artists notoriously struggle to make ends meet financially, but few of them question their calling. That type of clarity is more of a challenge for the rest of us, whether our collar is white or blue. For most, punching the time clock or donning a lab coat may pay the bills, but it doesn't look or feel like this elusive concept of calling.

In his book *The Call: Finding and Fulfilling the Central Purpose of Your Life*, Os Guinness, the great-great-great-grandson of legendary brewer Arthur Guinness, says our calling "is 'the ultimate why' for living, the highest source of purpose in human existence."[1]

As much as I enjoy Guinness's poetic description (and a pint of his forefathers' handiwork), I fear that its somewhat grandiose implications may intimidate the skeptics and doubters among us. So let's discern your calling through another simple set of steps.

What It Is

An activity, role, or pursuit might be your calling if the following are true:

1. You can say without hesitation, "I love doing this."
2. You're good at it.

3. It's life-giving—the activity generally doesn't tire you spiritually.
4. The activity is consistent with your values.
5. Your goals are complementary to your calling.
6. You've received recognition from multiple sources that this is "your thing."
7. It benefits others.

These first three points generally work together. When you love doing something, you're likely to do it as often as possible, allowing proficiency to become a natural by-product. When you love something and, in addition, you're good at it, the activity is also often life-giving. You labor but do not grow weary. You're in "the zone."

When you're good at doing something that is life-giving to you, the chances are favorable that the practice is born of your values and complementary to your life goals, but it's a great cross-check to gauge consistency at this stage of the process.

It can be difficult to objectively recognize our greatest talents because many of us, depending on our personalities or life experiences, magnify or discount our inherent strengths. It can be helpful in determining our calling, therefore, when others recognize it for us. "Wow! You're really a natural at [insert activity]." And just to ensure the compliment is more than an attempt by someone to motivate us into an action that will benefit them, it's best to have multiple qualified sources corroborate their opinion. Listen to unsolicited commendations from people who don't have a stake in your chosen path.

Finally, while most of the discernment process involves self-analysis, the very nature of a calling is that it's used for the benefit of others. We are called *to* something and *for* someone (or many).

What It's Not

Another great way to determine your calling is by acknowledging what it is not. A mentor of mine once admonished me for pursuing too many activities at once. Saying yes to everything had limited my ability to do the most good with the limited amount of time and energy at my disposal.

Simple Money Journal Entry

My mentor recommended a very simple exercise that I still use to this day. On a blank sheet of paper, he drew a line down the middle. At the top of the left-hand column, he wrote the phrase "Life-Giving." On the right column, he wrote "Life-Taking."

Life-Giving	Life-Taking

Then he had me pick a side on which to write down each of the numerous roles and obligations I had assumed were all somehow part of my calling. That I was capable of fulfilling any of these roles was beside the point. Instead, if there was anything I'd said yes to that seemed to slow the clock and sap my energy, it should likely be placed in the "Life-Taking" column. Those items were probably not part of my calling and should be the first on the chopping block when it came to seeking out a more livable life.

This is not to suggest, of course, that you simply shouldn't do anything that you'd prefer not to do in work or life. If you feel called to be a medical doctor, you're going to have a tough time living out your calling if you categorize scientific reading as a life-taking exercise. Indeed, in pursuit of our life-giving calling, most of us must labor through days, months, or even years of life-taking work on the path to fully living it.

Is a Calling Always a Job?

Speaking of work, the entire notion of a calling often seems synonymous with our formal work—our profession or our job. Is that the only option? No, I don't believe so.

While it may be ideal to find our calling in the primary way most of us spend our waking hours as adults—at our job—it's not a necessity. In fact, necessity requires many people to take any available work to pay the bills. They instead find their calling elsewhere, perhaps through coaching sports, heading up the PTA, or teaching Sunday school.

I know construction workers and plumbers who've found their calling in their day jobs, but I also know lawyers and doctors whose callings are outside of their well-established professions.

Can a Calling Change?

Michael Evans, the son of a proudly Irish member of the Chicago Fire Department, applied his entrepreneurial energies initially in his calling as a Chicago Mercantile Exchange commodities trader. You know, those guys who run around yelling at people all day, predicting the price direction of coffee beans and oranges? "Most days," Michael told me, "I returned home to my family tired and happy."

But the advance of global electronic trading predicted the end of traditional floor trading in the early 2000s. At the same time, an experience in a "safe" investment gone bad led Evans to serve as a lead plaintiff in a class-action suit against those responsible for what amounted to a collapsed Ponzi scheme. Michael began to envision Calling 2.0 in the form of a company he would start, offering personal financial guidance to individuals and families to help them avoid the pitfalls of investing that he's seen at very close range.

"Making the leap from a one-man show to forming—and being formed by—a personal wealth support team has been one of the most rewarding personal makeovers ever," said Evans. "It's been a little like the television show *Survivor* in reverse, where I've discovered that getting voted off my own little island was actually the best thing that could have happened for me and my family."

Yes, a calling can change. Sometimes it may even be forced upon us. But we must be careful not to confuse a shift in calling with resistance—the natural fear that seems to creep into those moments when we're on the precipice of stepping out boldly into our calling.

Does Everyone Have a Calling?

Which leaves us with the most challenging question in this vein: Does everyone have a calling, or is it for only a select few?

I believe with all of my heart that there is a calling out there for each of us, a lesson I learned the hard way.

In the summer of 1994, I was the stereotypical eighteen-year-old punk kid with a chip on his shoulder and a singular value, goal, *and* calling all wrapped into one—me, myself, and I. I was looking for Enough in all the wrong places.

After a day that was not particularly long or hard, basically twirling a whistle and perfecting my tan while working as a lifeguard at a community pool, I spent the evening playing a couple hours of volleyball and engaging in some activities of questionable wisdom.

My girlfriend wisely drove my car back to her parents' place, where I entered a deep slumber, until I was roused at 2:00 a.m. with this panicked reminder: "If my dad finds you here in the middle of the night, he'll kill us both!" I groggily sloughed to my 1988 Plymouth Horizon, bedecked with the stickers of classic rock bands, which never made it home that night.

I don't know exactly where on the road I fell asleep, but the rumble strip in the shoulder awakened me just in time to fully experience my car careening over a steep embankment. After rolling down the hill, the car landed on its wheels, and although I shunned the use of seat belts, I somehow landed back in the driver's seat.

But all was not well. My right leg was visibly broken and, unbeknownst to me, so was my pelvis. Fearing an explosion—because that's what happened in all of the *Lethal Weapon* and *Die Hard* movies so popular in that era—I scrambled to open the driver's side door, to no avail.

Over the course of the next four hours, through spans of unconsciousness, I flipped and flopped my way to every door in an unsuccessful attempt to escape. As the car had rolled down the hill, the metal had folded over each door.

Finally, I lay down in the backseat amidst the shattered glass, broken and bloodied, relinquishing my grasp on life.

Shortly after a truck driver spotted my car at dawn, I was awakened by the sound of metal being cut and bent to free me from the vehicle. The last thing I remember from the accident scene, as I was wheeled to the helicopter bound for the University of Maryland's legendary shock trauma unit, was the sound of a medic alerting his colleagues, "It doesn't look good—I don't think this kid's gonna make it."

His initial diagnosis would soon be confirmed. After reaching the hospital, my left lung collapsed. When my body began fighting the breathing tubes inserted into my chest, the doctors were forced to induce a life-saving coma, not knowing if or when I'd reemerge.

At one point, the medical staff warned my parents that my chances of living had fallen below 10 percent. Although visitors were not allowed in the intensive care unit, extended family and close friends were now invited to say their goodbyes.

I lived, and it is a testament to one of the best shock trauma units in the country. But it also defied the odds, a reality with which I struggled for more than a decade. It was a long and painful rehabilitation—especially since I ignored physical therapy—but it was the psychological and spiritual implications that plagued me the most.

I couldn't understand why I had been spared, of all people. I felt I didn't deserve it, and I practically resented the second chance. I didn't want to "do something with my life," and for several years I didn't.

My behavioral patterns became even more destructive and self-indulgent until one day, six years after the accident, I succumbed to the Reality that never stopped pursuing me—that there is a purpose for each of our lives, even mine.

It's up to us, however, as to if or how we pursue that purpose. Everybody has a calling, but not everyone finds it.

It's up to you.

Simple Money Calling Summary

1. The foundation of life planning, created by your values, is lived out in the form of pursuing your goals and culminates in your calling. This is the life-giving pursuit that makes you think, "I was *made* to do this!"

2. You might be living out your calling if the following are true:

   - You can say without hesitation, "I love doing this."
   - You're good at it.
   - It's life-giving—the activity generally doesn't "wear you out."
   - The activity is consistent with your values.
   - Your goals are complementary to your calling.
   - You've received recognition from multiple sources that this is "your thing."
   - It benefits others.

3. It's great if your calling lines up with your job, but that's not the only option. You might find it in another context.

4. Everybody has a calling, but not everyone finds it.

What INSIGHTS and ACTIONS did you take from this chapter?

5

TIME

Investing Your Most Precious Commodity

WHY do I need to read this chapter?

You know you want Enough. Finding the motivation to craft goals that rest on top of a foundation created from your personal values sounds fantastic. And what's more inspiring than finding and living out your calling? There's only one problem—you have only so much time.

Our emotional brain—the Elephant—isn't lazy. It's exhausted. More money might help ease the burden, but we can always make more money. Our time, however, is a daily gift that expires immediately. Our most valuable commodity, our most precious investment, therefore, is time.

I see a lot of financially successful people who don't have Enough be-cause life is frantic. They articulate values—but to them they're just words they heard on a commercial. Their goals are limited to those set *for* them at work. Their calling is their calendar and email inbox.

If this resonates, I recommend reading this chapter, which is an attempt to bring the concept of values we discussed in the first four chapters into our daily reality. The key, as you will see, is not to fully embrace someone else's time management strategy, even if it has worked for them, but to customize your own strategy in a way that will work for you.

The Recipe for Failure

Ironically, I have tried more productivity systems and tools than could possibly be productive. Stephen Covey's *7 Habits* are deservedly legendary, and I'm better for every habit I'm able to employ. David Allen's Getting Things Done (GTD) methodology was even more helpful for me, especially because it seems to hone the best of Covey's principles to a more elegant simplicity. But both of their complete, proprietary systems proved too much for me to maintain long term.

After keeping up for a few weeks—even past the twenty-one days that supposedly cements a new habit—I always failed to maintain the system. You know the story: a reliably random task turns into a seemingly wasted day followed by a week of piled emails and unfulfilled pledges (and all of the guilt and shame to boot).

Another reason I've failed to maintain well-meaning time management systems is that after the initial novelty wore off, the checklists and to-dos all seemed to become rote and, well, boring. Most time management systems are very Rider-centric (see chap. 3), and I needed to get the Elephant in the game to make it stick. I needed something more visual and engaging to hold my attention.

Then Ryan Carson, the founder of Treehouse,[1] introduced me to Trello (via blogger Leo Babauta). Trello is a highly visual (free) online collaborative project management tool, with access online and on iOS and Android devices. Carson reengineered it to become his go-to personal task management system.

I've been using it for almost three years now without fail, synthesizing everything that stuck with me from Covey and Allen, along with Carson and Babauta's wisdom, to create the only task management system that's ever really worked for me. Here's how it works for me and could work for you:

A Visual System: Invest Your Time Wisely

Create Your Own System in Seven Steps

1. *After creating a Trello account, create a new "board" and call it "Tasks."* Each board is composed of vertical "lists"—these will function as your task prioritization system. Then, each new "card" you add to a List represents an individual task.

2. *Create your lists.* My lists are a conglomeration of what I've learned from Covey's *7 Habits* and Allen's GTD. My first list, on the left, is called "Priorities." It includes what I most

value in life and what I want to consume the majority of my time. Next is "Today," the list of items I hope to accomplish today, followed by "Incoming," new tasks that have yet to be prioritized. As you might guess, "This Week" houses the tasks I hope to accomplish this week. "Later" includes the tasks I'd like to get to eventually but are not yet urgent. "Waiting On" are those tasks I've accomplished but require action on another person's part. "Done" is a list of the tasks I've accomplished that day.

3. *Whether you call it Priorities, Big Rocks (Covey), or Big Picture (Carson), or Most Important (Babauta), create a list under that heading with your biggest priorities in life.* Mine are Spiritual, Family, Health, Writing/Speaking, Business, and Personal. Now click on your first prioritization category listed. You'll see an option to "Edit Labels." I recommend making each of your Priorities a specific color. Clicking "Change Label Titles" will allow you to also give each color a name corresponding with your Priorities. Now, each time you add a new task, you can color-code it with an appropriate label.

4. *Add tasks.* If you're importing tasks from another system or just want to do a brain dump, add all of your tasks to the Incoming list and *then* decide where to put them later. Click "Add a card . . ." at the bottom of the appropriate list and type a brief description of the task to be performed. Before you even hit the green "Add" button, hit the dropdown in the bottom right corner and that will give you the option to add a label. Once the task is added, a host of new options can be seen by clicking on the card itself. Here you can give the task a longer description, create a checklist within the task, attach a file, or give it a due date. Preferring the GTD approach (chap. 3), I keep it simple and trust my daily prioritization ritual.

5. *After adding a bunch of new tasks, it's time to prioritize each one by placing it in the appropriate list.* Simply click

and drag the card with the task you'd like to prioritize and move it to the appropriate list. If your lists reach beyond the edge of your screen, you can hover on the screen's edge and watch the board traverse in that direction, allowing you to place the card in the list of your choosing. You can also grab and drag the screen in any direction you choose.

6. *The one essential habit you must form for this—or any other task management system—to work is to review your tasks board each morning.* Ryan Carson recommends taking 19 minutes to start every day organizing your to-dos. "Limiting this to 19 minutes," he says, "keeps you focused and ensures you don't spend all your time prioritizing instead of doing."[2] First, add any meetings or calls on your calendar that day to Today with a precursor (M) for meetings and (C) for calls, along with the time. Then, relocate new Incoming tasks to the appropriate list. Review This Week to determine which tasks should be completed Today. Then, review Later to see which tasks should be bumped up to This Week. Scan Waiting On to determine if you need to nudge someone else. Only keep tasks that were completed in the Done list for a single day, purging this list each morning by either moving the task to Waiting On or archiving it. You can archive individual tasks by clicking on the card's dropdown, or you can "Archive All Cards in This List" by hitting the list's dropdown in the upper right-hand corner.

7. *Now, the fun part—getting things Done.* If you spent 19 minutes reviewing your board in the morning, you shouldn't need to look at any lists except for Today and Done for the remainder of the day. (You should also be freed from your calendar.) Throughout the course of your day, move completed cards to Done and reprioritize Today, leaving the next action to be performed at the top.

Email: Friend or Foe?

One of the perpetual faux-tasks that can lead many of us astray from the completion of actual tasks is constant attention to our email. As Claire Díaz-Ortiz reminds us, "Email isn't work."[3] It certainly feels like it, but email is more a conduit leading us to tasks than it is a task in itself. An email inbox is also a horrendous task management venue because it distracts us from the next task on our priority list. But we do often send and receive tasks through email, so Trello provides us with an answer:

Hit "Show sidebar" in the top right of your Trello screen. Under the Menu header, click on Settings, then click on Email settings. This will allow you to copy and paste a specific email address for sending emailed tasks from your inbox to the board and list of your choosing. (Be sure to create a contact for that email address—something like Trello Tasks—and you won't have to remember the email address.)

Trello is intended to be an interactive project management solution for groups, but it has become my highly individualized, personal task management system of choice. The interactive, visual nature of Trello is what attracted me to it and has kept me using it. But the best part about it is that you can create your *own* system within Trello (or some other great systems, like DropTask and Todoist).

Time Is More Precious Than Money

As the Fed has taught us, the potential supply of US dollars is limitless (sarcasm intended). Even for most of us individually, we are capable, to varying degrees, of generating money through work, investment, and happenstance.

Time, however, is a different story.

It brings to mind these lyrics: "Where you invest your love, you invest your life," croons Marcus Mumford in "Awake My Soul."

Sure, musicians are notorious for writing lyrics because they sound self-important, or maybe simply because they rhyme, but Mumford has earned a reputation for lyrical brilliance and offers us something deep and meaningful here to apply in our lives and finances.

No matter how much we strive, delegate, and engineer for efficiency, there are only twenty-four hours in each day. We are unable to manufacture more time, and once a moment has passed, it is beyond retrieval.

Of these twenty-four hours each day, if we assume that we will sleep, work, and commute for approximately seventeen of them, that leaves us with a meager seven hours to apply ourselves to loftier pursuits. After an hour at the gym, an hour to eat, and another hour to decompress with a book or television show, we're down to four measly hours. That's only four hours to personally affect the people we are presumably working and staying healthy for—those we love.

Our human capacity to love also has its limits.

How Would You Invest Your Love?

While not measurable, we can all acknowledge that our capacity to love, in the four hours each day that we have to directly invest it, is affected by how we've invested the other twenty hours. By the "end" of many days, we are just beginning our four hours, and we are already spent. Even if we wanted to, we have nothing left to give—no love left to invest.

I am a chief offender of misallocating my love.

I often allow the four hours I have to give to my wife, Andrea, and two boys, Kieran and Connor, to shrink to three, two, or even one. In whatever time is allocated, I often serve leftover love, having over-invested myself throughout the day. Then I steal from their time, interrupting it with "important" emails and calls.

I must acknowledge that these are choices I make.

We have the choice to order our loves, to acknowledge the limited nature of time and our own capacity, and to prioritize our work and life.

It's entirely appropriate to love our work and the people we serve through it. It's entirely appropriate to love ourselves and to do what is necessary to be physically, fiscally, psychologically, and spiritually healthy. It's entirely appropriate to love the areas in which we live out service and civic duty, and to serve there well. Therefore, almost paradoxically, it's entirely appropriate to spend 83 percent of our daily allotment of time in pursuits other than the direct edification of those we love the most.

But what would our lives look like if we engineered our days to make the very most of those other four hours?

Would we have a different job? Would we live in a different house or part of the country? Would we drive a different car? Would we say no to some people more and to other people less? Would we invest our time and money differently?

How will you invest your love?

Simple Money Time Management Summary

1. Our most valuable commodity—our most precious investment—is time.

2. The optimal productivity tool is the one that *you* design.

3. Using a visual time management system helps enlist the Elephant in the battle for adoption. Trello provides an excellent tool that can be used for this purpose.

4. Email isn't work.

5. "Where you invest your love, you invest your life."

What INSIGHTS and ACTIONS did you take from this chapter?

PART 2

PLANNING FOR TODAY

The most important elements of personal finance are, thankfully, the simplest—but they're not easy.

6

PERSPECTIVE

Where Do You Stand?

WHY do I need to read this chapter?

It's impossible to know how to get where you're going if you don't know where you are. You know a lot more about yourself—your motivations, values, goals, and hopefully even your calling—after engaging this book's foundational chapters. But now it's time to see where you stand financially, whether the situation is good, bad, or ugly.

We'll take a snapshot of your financial landscape through the lens of the Enough Index, giving you a clear answer to an important question I know you're asking: "So, how am I doing?"

I think you may know the answer in your gut, but the Enough Index will help explain why.

Savings Index

We will focus on four numbers to gauge your household's financial health through a single, simple numerical score. The first number represents your financial safety margin from, well, life. It's your money moat.

Do you have a money moat?

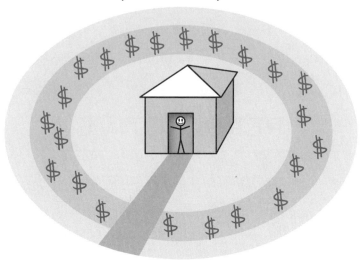

How much cash do you have on hand that is not already pledged to a creditor or near-term savings goal, like the down payment on a home or a car purchase? Often referred to as an emergency reserve, this is the buffer between you and the chief Enough buster, Revolving Unsecured Consumer (RUC) debt. More on that shortly.

Your amount of cash reserves is the best indicator of your financial stress level in the *present*, right this very minute. If your income *this month* goes to pay *this month's* bills, you're living paycheck to paycheck. I don't have to remind you that this is stressful.

If you have a month's worth of savings, you can breathe. But you're not likely to outlast a major household emergency financially or survive a job loss. If you have three months' worth of living expenses to serve as financial fortification, it's a good sign that you live below your means. If you have six months' worth of living expenses or more in cash, you have built yourself a nice layer of financial independence that no doubt helps you sleep better at night. Can you see how key this is in pursuit of Enough (chap. 1)?

How many months' worth of living expenses do you have in emergency reserves? _____

Please multiply the above number by 8: _____ x 8

YOUR SAVINGS INDEX: ☐

Debt Index

The second number we'll use to gauge your financial health is more of a red flag. It's the amount of Revolving Unsecured Consumer (RUC) debt you owe that *won't be paid off at the end of the month*. And yes, I made up this acronym.

- It's *revolving* debt as opposed to installment debt. Installment debt has a set number of payments after which the debt will be repaid in full. Most home mortgages are installment debt, as are most auto loans and student loans. Conversely, most credit cards are lines of credit that, like flesh-eating zombies, limp into perpetuity until you annihilate them. You'll have a minimum payment that adjusts according to the amount of outstanding debt and is primarily designed to *keep you in debt*.

- It's *unsecured* debt as opposed to secured debt. A mortgage is, by definition, a secured loan. It's secured by the home on which the bank can foreclose if you don't meet your end of the bargain—to make regular mortgage payments. An auto loan is also by definition secured, whereas a credit card and most consumer loans are not.

- It's *consumer* debt as opposed to commercial debt. Commercial debt is for businesses. Consumer debt is for individuals and households. A commercial loan can certainly have a meaningful impact on your business, but it does not directly threaten your personal assets. Retail credit cards are a great example of RUC debt.

In most cases, your RUC debt number is simply how much you have in credit card debt, and it tells the story of your *financial past*. It represents either bad luck or bad decisions (or both).

There are understandable reasons for having RUC debt. For example, a job loss, divorce, or disability. But in most cases, it's a sign of financial instability or, at least, unpreparedness. And, even in the case of a financial surprise like those I just mentioned, a financially fortified household need not resort to RUC debt.

RUC debt is not the only variety of toxic household debt, and all forms of debt will be accounted for in the next chapter. However, RUC debt is the ultimate Enough buster for at least three important reasons: (1) It's like the Energizer bunny—it just keeps going and going and going. And that's quite by design. (2) It also has notoriously high interest rates, usually well into double digits and often more than 20 percent, which only strengthens its endurance. (3) But most importantly, while your mortgage may represent a housing problem, your high auto loan a vehicle problem, and your student loan an education problem, RUC debt is intensely personal and eats away at us on an individual level. It feels like a *you* problem, symbolizing personal financial failure.

Are you still paying for (and punishing yourself for) past financial mistakes?

How many months' worth of living expenses do you have tied up in RUC debt? _____

Please multiply the above number by 10: _____ x 10

YOUR DEBT INDEX: [ ]

Retirement Index

Once we've dug out of our past and raised our gaze from the present, we can consider the *future*. In saving for retirement, we're really deferring a portion of our salary today to ensure that we have a sufficient income stream in the years after we stop working, whether by choice or by force.

What is your retirement readiness at this stage of the journey? Fidelity Investments pulled together some analysis[1] and simplified the concept of retirement readiness by giving us benchmarks based on our age and current salary:

Fidelity Retirement Scorecard

Are you on track for retirement savings?

If you are this old . . .	. . . you should have this much saved.
30	0.5 × current salary
35	1 ×
40	2 ×
45	3 ×
50	4 ×
55	5 ×
60	6 ×
65	7 ×
67	8 ×

SOURCE: Fidelity Investments[2]

According to the study, you're on track if you, for example, have half of your current salary saved for retirement at age thirty or four times your salary at age fifty. Yes, this is an oversimplification upon which we'll expand a great deal more in chapters 11 and 12, dedicated to the topic of retirement. But for now, where do you stand based on Fidelity's matrix?

Let's figure out what percentage of Fidelity's target you have reached at this point. Here's the formula:

What is your retirement readiness score?

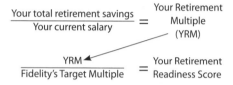

$$\frac{\text{Your total retirement savings}}{\text{Your current salary}} = \begin{array}{c}\text{Your Retirement} \\ \text{Multiple} \\ \text{(YRM)}\end{array}$$

$$\frac{\text{YRM}}{\text{Fidelity's Target Multiple}} = \begin{array}{c}\text{Your Retirement} \\ \text{Readiness Score}\end{array}$$

Mathematically, you take the multiple of the income you have saved (Your Retirement Multiple) and divide it by Fidelity's corresponding multiple for your age. For example, if you're forty and only have one times the amount of your salary saved when you're supposed to have two times your income, your answer would be 0.5. Whereas, if you're fifty-five and have seven times your current salary saved, versus the recommended five, your score would be 1.4.

How much of your future income needs have you funded?

What is your Retirement Readiness Score? _____

Please multiply your score by 56: _____ x 56

YOUR RETIREMENT INDEX: ☐

By the way, if you're off the Fidelity grid because you're under the age of thirty, here's how to compute your Retirement Index: Take the percentage of your income you're currently saving annually into retirement accounts and multiply that number by 5.6. For example, if you're saving 5 percent of your income (5 x 5.6) your Retirement Index is 28. If you're saving 10 percent of your income, your Retirement Index is 56.

Giving Index

While your current level of financial health requires multiple indicators for accuracy, your overall financial *satisfaction* may be best gauged in a single number—the percentage of your income that you give away each year.

I must first disclaim that giving out of compulsion or guilt, in which case the personal benefits of giving are likely diminished or eliminated, may actually signify a misfiring Money Script (chap. 1) or even a financial disorder. But someone who gives healthily does so precisely because he or she has gained Enough.

Here are three reasons why giving may benefit the giver as much, or more, than the recipient:

1. Personally, you'll feel good. Apparently we are "wired" to receive a physiological benefit from giving. It creates the same sense of satisfaction you get from a compliment from your friend or a raise from your boss. In addition to this individual sense of satisfaction, you will likely feel a greater sense of control over your own financial situation when you give to others. This positive response is especially heightened when you are able to connect yourself physically—not just fiscally—in this act of giving.

2. Practically, you'll save money on your taxes. When you give to a qualified charitable organization, you will generally receive an income tax deduction, putting money back in your pocket for your willingness to give. Talk to your CPA to see how this will affect you personally.

3. Mysteriously, you'll actually have more money. Once in a pattern of giving, you will likely develop a heightened sense of the needs of others and the excess in your own budget. The net effect is that you may find yourself choosing to purchase one or two fewer $5 lattes per week and staying in more often

instead of going out. The result is more money in your bank account.

To what degree are you taking advantage of these benefits?

What percentage of your income do you give on an annual basis? _____

Please multiply this number by 2: _____ x 2

YOUR GIVING INDEX: [_____]

Enough Index

Okay, now let's put all of these numbers together to arrive at your Enough Index:

Simple Money Journal Entry

Enough Index

Savings Index: _____

Subtract your Debt Index: − _____

Add your Retirement Index: + _____

Add your Giving Index: + _____

YOUR ENOUGH INDEX: [_____]

The Enough Index is designed to yield a 100-point score if you have a "textbook" three months of living expenses saved, no RUC debt, your retirement saving is on track per Fidelity's retirement analysis, and you're giving away 10 percent of your income to causes outside your home. It's not a "best-case" scenario, but it is quite stable.

To demonstrate how the weighting is handled, here's what the "textbook" example referred to above would look like:

Savings:	3 months x	8	=	24 points
Debt:	0 months x	10	=	0 points against
Retirement:	1 (100%) x	56	=	56 points
Giving:	10 (%) x	2	=	20 points
				100 points

If you have two months of savings (2 x 8) less one month's worth of debt (1 x 10) plus 1.3 times the Fidelity retirement scale (1.3 x 56) and you give 5 percent of your annual income to charity (5 x 2), your aggregate Enough Index score would be 88.8.

On the other hand, let's say you have six months of expenses saved (6 x 8), no debt, you register 0.8 on the Fidelity retirement scale (0.8 x 56), and you give away 12 percent (12 x 2) of your income. In this case, you'd register a 116.8. As you can see, much like the National Football League's "passer rating," it's not a 100-point scale.

What about a scenario that I fear is more likely the norm? Living paycheck to paycheck earns zero points, while having three months' worth of expenses in debt will drop you below zero to −30. Perhaps you have 50 percent of what Fidelity recommends—a retirement score of 0.5, worth 28 Enough points—and heck no, you can't give anything. You feel like a charity case yourself! And that's exactly what your −2 Enough Index score is designed to reflect—how content you feel.

You'll note that each feature is not equally weighted. RUC debt hurts more than cash savings help, and quite purposefully. The emotional damage RUC debt imposes can weigh heavily on us. This is why I would recommend in most cases that surplus emergency savings be used to pay off RUC debt. Indeed, paying an exorbitant interest rate *is* a financial emergency.

Some will certainly argue that *not* considering excessive mortgage, automobile, and student loan debt is shortsighted, and I'm sure there are a number of exceptions for which this is true. However, because these loans are installment debt and two are secured, they would not have the damaging financial or emotional characteristics of RUC debt. And, if the payments are unduly burdensome in those cases, it's likely to be reflected in their inability to maintain cash reserves and adequately save for retirement.

Being on track for retirement, meanwhile, is weighted very heavily. This is because problems like cash deficiencies, burdensome debt, and lackluster giving, while painful, can be remedied in the relative short term. Or, at least, shorter term. And precisely because long-term investing offers us the benefit of compounded growth, this means too little retirement savings is a compounding dilemma. It's much harder to catch up, especially as we age.

It is vitally important to understand this is not a measurement of personal worth or value, and it's not a competition. Your score is simply designed to reflect how it feels to be you, financially speaking. And only financially speaking.

It measures the degree to which money is serving you, versus you serving it.

Selfish Generosity

Some may criticize me for weighting charitable giving so heavily, or even at all, as a measurement of financial stability. Please don't consider my plea for generosity as sermonizing or judgmental. Yes, I do believe that there is an element of duty here, and that those who have more are called to give to those less fortunate, but my primary message regarding giving is that it will benefit you, personally, on your path to Enough.

And I don't speak as someone who has always given generously or never suffered financially.

From the moment my wife and I were married, we committed to giving roughly 10 percent of our income to charity. We simply made the decision to live off of 90 percent of our income and we never really questioned it. Until.

When I established myself as a self-employed financial advisor, my wife became the primary breadwinner. My income ranged from zero to not much—every month—for close to two years. In the middle of that stretch, we were blessed with the birth of our first son.

Since before we were married, my wife's plan was to sacrifice her promising career to be a stay-at-home mom, and I fully supported her in this endeavor. The only problem was that now we had numerous financial commitments—foremost among them, a mortgage—and far less of an ability to satisfy them without my wife's income.

Incidentally, as a guy with the "My primary role is to provide and protect" Money Script (chap. 1), you can imagine how demoralizing—I mean, educational—this period of time was for me.

Have no doubt. We seriously considered the good sense behind maintaining our pledge to give away the first 10 percent of our income when our reserves dipped into the single digits and we didn't know when the next cash infusion would come. But we pulled through.

I'm not ready to suggest that we pulled through *because* we continued to give. That's a topic for another chapter in another book. But there is no question that we were buoyed personally by maintaining our giving through a trying financial drought.

Yet, somehow, we forgot that valuable life lesson.

Years later, even in the midst of our most profitable year to date as a family, we made a decision to reach financially for a new house. You know, the one with the acre of yard nestling the idyllic center-hall Colonial with room to frolic for both our two boys and soon-to-be-purchased family dog?

The only problem was that the house was a bit of a fixer-upper, and required a significant amount of work (read: money) to even come close to the ideal. To pull it off, we'd need to substantially reduce our annual giving for six months—a year, max. A small "sacrifice," right?

That one-year period turned into several years. They were some of our best financially, but our giving (and our saving, for that matter) were down.

We had more income and more assets, but we didn't *feel* as prosperous.

We had more, but it wasn't Enough.

The Enough Index isn't close to perfect, and it's not designed to be. It's designed to measure the elements of our financial lives that tend to give, *and strip*, us of contentment.

I invite you, if you haven't already, to put it to the test. Reflect on your own financial situation. When you have, it's time to move on to a more practical discussion about managing the two most essential elements of every financial plan—savings and debt. We'll do so in our next chapter by examining exactly how much you need in savings and how to manage debt.

Simple Money Index Summary

1. In order to gauge where you stand financially, we examine four numbers:

   - *Your Savings Index*—Your emergency reserves are an indicator of the present state of your finances.

   - *Your Debt Index*—Your amount of Revolving Unsecured Consumer (RUC) debt—typically credit card debt—is an indicator of your past financial decisions.

   - *Your Retirement Index*—The amount you've saved for retirement, relative to your current salary, demonstrates how well you've prepared for the future.

- *Your Giving Index*—The amount you freely give measures the degree to which money is serving you versus you serving it.

2. The combination of each of these indices culminates in your Enough Index score, which is both a measure of your practical financial health and the degree to which you have attained Enough.

What INSIGHTS and ACTIONS did you take from this chapter?

7

ESSENTIALS

Straight Talk on Savings and Debt

WHY do I need to read this chapter?

In the previous chapter, we discussed taking stock of your overall financial picture and the important roles that savings and debt play. They are opposite sides of the same coin. After all, why would one willingly go into credit card debt if sufficient savings were available?

In this chapter, we'll broaden the discussion to consider the topics of savings and debt more practically. How much should you keep in savings, assuming you can get past living paycheck to paycheck? We'll also discuss the primary forms of debt, including the degree to which they help or hurt us financially, and answer the often-asked question, "Is there good debt, like school loans and mortgages?"

But what's even more important than addressing the outward signs of financial mismanagement is discerning your fundamental financial disposition. What is your cash flow personality? Are you a Saver or a Spender? Or perhaps you're one of the more extreme, a Hoarder or a Spendthrift.

Let's find out.

Savers and Hoarders

Are you naturally inclined to live below your means? If so, you might be a Saver. Savers are predisposed to storing up cash as opposed to spending it. They typically have this proclivity hard-wired early in life as represented in their Money Scripts (chap. 1).

But there is another type of household prone to building up cash, and it's not always a good thing. Some are Hoarders. Hoarders can't save enough money. The "I-can-never-have-enough-cash" Money Script can rise to the level of a money disorder. For some, it's a control issue. But for many, especially from the Great Depression era, it's more about fear.

Several years ago, I received a phone call from an elderly woman who was audibly concerned. Grace had heard me on the radio and was concerned that a representative of her bank had unnecessarily sold her an annuity in which she invested $100,000. She asked me to review the policy and give her a second opinion. I told her I would be glad to, and gave her the address to my office. Sheepishly, she responded, "But I don't drive the beltway."

I wasn't going to rescind my promise, so I asked Grace for her address and set out, in my mind, on a charitable venture. Based on her address, I thought that $100,000 in Grace's annuity represented the whole of her life savings. I rapped on her hollow front door, looking left and right a bit apprehensively. She lived in a notoriously bad part of town.

Grace was right. The annuity she'd been sold was entirely inappropriate. It had a seven-year surrender charge, the period in which withdrawals could be penalized. Heck, at her age Grace wasn't even buying green bananas! Fortunately, we were still within Maryland's "20-day penalty-free" period, so I accompanied her to the bank to demand her money back.

Thereafter, Grace divulged that the hundred grand in the annuity didn't represent the totality of her life savings. As it turned out, not even close. She actually had $3.5 *million* in investments, most of it in the form of US savings bonds hidden behind the curtains of her run-down row home (which had been robbed multiple times).

Grace had been widowed for more than sixty years. She worked as a legal assistant until she was seventy without ever taking a single day of vacation. She saved every penny she possibly could and invested it in the safest vehicles she knew. Her Money Script—that she could never have enough money—was rooted in her intense fear of Depression-era loss.

My office practically adopted Grace. We helped her sell her house and move into a comfortable assisted living facility, but her fear could not be broken. When she died at eighty-seven, she had no heirs and left more than a million dollars to three different charities. Sadly, she never knew what it was like to live with Enough.

How Much Is Too Much?

Too much? Well, that's a good problem to have, isn't it? Conventional wisdom says three months of living expenses—the standard we used in the Enough Index (chap. 6)—is how much you should have in emergency savings. But there are four factors that play into this decision:

1. The number of income streams coming into a household.
2. The variability of income streams.
3. The volatility of income sources.
4. The sleep-at-night factor.

If a household has more than one income stream, emergency reserves are a hedge against a job loss or reduction in compensation. Salaried employees have a less variable stream of income than a person who receives a meaningful part of their compensation from discretionary bonuses. Someone who receives a meaningful part of their compensation from discretionary bonuses has a less variable stream of income than a person whose compensation is based solely on eat-what-you-kill commissions.

The volatility of income sources is driven by the stability of the company and the industry it represents. A tenured professor has more stability than a mortgage banker. A mortgage banker has more stability than a self-employed dog walker.

The sleep-at-night factor takes us back, again, to our emotional motivation. If having $50,000 cash in the bank helps you get to sleep five minutes faster, who am I to judge? (If your number is $500,000, however, we might need to talk.) Remember, personal finance is more personal than it is finance. When the Elephant and the Rider (chap. 3) go head-to-head, the Elephant always wins.

How, then, do we translate the above four financial stability factors into an appropriate emergency reserve calculation? There's no magic, and as is so much of personal finance, it's as much art as it is science. In the end, though, it should probably range from two to twelve months of living expenses.

If your household has two tenured professors, you're part of the minority that can slide by with a couple months' worth of reserves. If your family of five is supported only by a single self-employed income stream, try to have at least a year's worth of living expenses saved up. Most of us would ideally be between three and six months.

Degrees of Independence

But there's another way to look at emergency reserves, and it may lead you to consider setting the bar even higher if you're able. By increasing your emergency savings, you're actually buying yourself degrees of financial independence, which could totally change your outlook on work.

When most people think about the term "financial independence," they're thinking of retirement. They're thinking about having enough money saved so that they don't need to work at all. But what if you had enough money saved to buy yourself a three-month sabbatical? Or what if you could take the next six months to retool and change careers? A year to teach snorkeling in Costa Rica?

My friend Tim Donohue began his career about fifteen years ago, self-employed in the mortgage business. He knew he was in a volatile industry. He could easily break six figures in a good year and qualify for food stamps in the next.

He saw his colleagues spending every last penny in the good years, thinking that it would keep raining money indefinitely. But Tim knew better. A couple years into his career, he set his annual spending at the average between a big year and a bust year. That's what he lived on. Then, he dedicated himself to saving up a full year's worth of living expenses. In a few years, he was there. Then, he got to *two* years' worth of expenses.

Now, fifteen years into his career, thanks to healthy cash reserves, Tim is working because he wants to, not because he has to. His peers are the perpetually busy majority, scraping and clawing to keep up with their mortgage, 2.5 kids, and black Lab. But Tim has a different outlook on life and work. He's certainly not 100 percent financially independent. Not even close. But he's reached a meaningful degree of financial independence that has changed the way he views work, money, and life.

Months—Plural??

What if all this talk about having "months" of savings sounds ridiculous because you're like the majority of American households, who have approximately 0.005 months' worth of emergency cash reserves saved?

What if you're living paycheck to paycheck?

Well, you need only one month's worth of living expenses saved to get out of that certified cycle of stress. Jesse Mecham, founder of YNAB (YouNeedABudget.com), has created a system that is specifically designed to conquer the paycheck-to-paycheck, human-sized hamster wheel by simply getting one month ahead. The goal, and inevitable reality, is to have this month's income paying next month's bills. We'll hear more from Jesse in chapter 8.

Most people aren't going to go from having zero months of expenses saved to having three or six, but anyone with an income can find a way to get one month ahead, and eventually another. And so on.

How Should It Be Invested?

How should your emergency reserves be invested? Well, emergencies are inherently urgent, requiring you to access the money immediately. Therefore, an FDIC-insured savings account is likely the best option. At today's interest rates, I realize that using the word "invested" is an embellishment, but the safety of these funds is a priority over the potential for growth.

"Cash has an important place in the plan, and it isn't about making money directly," says Joe Pitzl, Managing Partner of Pitzl Financial. "Indirectly, it often leads to more money from less stress, and an ability to take different kinds of risks," such as a career move.

Consider using an online bank to warehouse your emergency reserves. Since most don't have brick-and-mortar overhead to support, they often offer higher interest rates than the big banks with endless commercials on television.

But what if you're fortunate enough to have a significant amount of emergency reserves, enough that it feels like you should be earning more than a savings account rate? First, congratulations. Second, it's now likely time to open a liquid investment account, if you don't already have one. To which, most people say, "Huh?"

I'm really just talking about a regular brokerage account, preferably a low-cost brokerage account with a reputable company. It's "liquid" in that, unlike retirement accounts and education savings plans, the money has no penalties associated with taking early distributions. There may, however, be tax consequences, so consult your tax preparer.

Think about it this way: You have special buckets—like IRAs and 401(k)s, our topic in chapter 11—that are set aside specifically for the future. Your emergency fund is purposefully accessible so that it can be used in the short term if necessary. If your emergency savings start spilling out over the top, your liquid, taxable brokerage account becomes your mid-term savings. You should be able to access your short-term savings in a day, your mid-term savings in three to five days, and ideally you'll consider your long-term savings off limits.

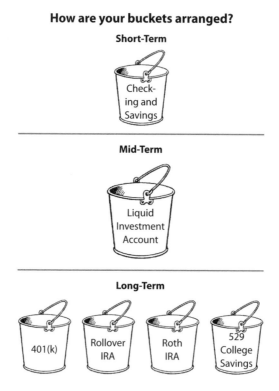

How are your buckets arranged?

Short-Term

Checking and Savings

Mid-Term

Liquid Investment Account

Long-Term

401(k)   Rollover IRA   Roth IRA   529 College Savings

Financial Peace

"Should I pay my mortgage off?"

A thirtysomething client came to me and asked for advice specific to his home mortgage. He was fortunate enough to have received a significant inheritance, but he'd never imagined having the ability to pay off his mortgage only a few years into buying the home. This was the home where he and his wife intended to raise their children.

Interest rates were low. He fully expected he could make more in a wisely diversified investment portfolio than the interest rate he was paying over the long term. So why even consider paying off the mortgage?

Peace.

I'd worked with enough clients, most of them older, who were privileged to be at a place in life where they too were blessed to consider this dilemma. They had enough money to be financially independent, but still retained a relatively small mortgage. Not all of them accepted this advice, but I recommended that they consider the intangible benefits of paying off their last remaining tangible debt.

Those who did, invariably came back to explain the mere act of paying off the last of their debt was an invigorating experience with ongoing benefits. Now they fully owned all of their assets. No one held anything over them financially.

Debt is clearly an Enough buster, but as it turns out, being debt-free is an Enough booster.

After running the numbers, I concluded that my thirtysomething client was similarly positioned. He could responsibly keep the mortgage and invest the payoff, or he could pay off the mortgage with little fear that it would negatively impact his long-term planning.

He chose to pay it off. A couple months later, he called specifically to say how much of a personal benefit he and his wife had derived from this financial decision.

And fortunately, this was a family of Savers. They were going to warehouse the cash they saved from not having a mortgage and use it to further fortify their family financially.

Spenders and Spendthrifts

If those who are predisposed to storing up cash are Savers and, to the extreme, Hoarders, what do we call those whose tendencies bend more toward evacuating cash? These are Spenders and, in some cases, Spendthrifts.

Spenders suffer to keep cash around. They are prone to considering everyday splurges an "emergency." Their talk about money is couched in optimism for a successful financial future. Spenders aren't necessarily addicted to debt, but because they soak up cash so prolifically, there's none left for emergencies. This can give a Spender license to interpret a dip into debt as an anomalous occurrence—not their fault. And occasionally, it's not.

A friend of mine, a single teacher known for her ebullient personality and mad karaoke chops, came to me recently. She had $7,000 of RUC debt she acknowledges she incurred for less-than-charitable reasons. She didn't think that would be a horribly burdensome amount. After all, it was just barely above the national average for her demographic.[1] Unfortunately, the interest rate on the loan is so high that she can't keep up with the minimum payments. "It's like twenty something," she told me.

"It was stupid, but c'mon!" she said. "I called them to ask if they would work with me on lowering the payment, but they said they couldn't while the account was in 'good standing.' So let me get this straight. I've got to stop paying my credit card bill and destroy my credit just to negotiate a better payment?"

Yep.

Now, by following the credit card company's mandated default-in-order-to-restructure policy, she's getting dehumanizing phone calls daily, reminding her of how much she failed financially.

Good Debt, Bad Debt?

"Is there good debt and bad debt?" Such is the debt question du jour, which I'm often asked, but it's the wrong question. It's like asking if there are good Yankees fans and bad Yankees fans. No, there are just Yankees fans. Of course, some of them are better than others. Some, we can live with; others—like RUC debt—are so obnoxious that we just need to "get riduvem."

Instead, think of debt this way. There's not good debt, just bad debt and better debt. It's a sliding scale ranging from RUC debt all the way up to a fixed-interest, low-interest, shorter-term home mortgage.

Bad debt / better debt continuum

BAD	RUC Debt	Margin Loan	Auto Loan	School Loan	HELOC	Traditional Home Mortgage	BETTER
	Occasionally necessary, never preferable	Don't touch	Use only in a pinch, pay off early	Better than no school, but not a debt license	Only for emergencies and short-term liquidity	Better than any other debt	

It's easier to say, "Debt is always bad, always wrong. Pay it off, or else you're stupid!" But that's simplistic, not simple. The absolutist's path certainly saves on word count, but it ignores the nuances and denies real life. Let's explore the debt continuum in more detail:

- *RUC debt*, as we've discussed, is occasionally necessary, but never preferable. It's an Enough buster and every effort should be made to pay it off. Yesterday.

- *Margin loans* are a form of debt secured by market investments (like stocks, bonds, and mutual funds) for the purpose of buying more securities. It is nothing short of dangerous. While history tells us that the market always goes up over long periods of time, there's no guarantee of that, especially in the short term. And when securities lose big—which they do—margin loans are "called" in and you have to come up with the cash. It's like betting on the market.

99

- *Auto loans* deserve the terrible reputation given to them, especially when used flippantly or habitually. But they're not inherently unhealthy. The primary reason they're a bad idea is because they are debt on a depreciating asset—an asset that loses value over time. They soak up cash flow that you could invest in appreciating assets or otherwise enjoy employing. Auto loans should be used only in a pinch, and paid off early, for two reasons: (1) The devaluation of automobiles happens so quickly that if you have a five-year loan—the norm—you'll likely be upside down as the depreciation of the vehicle outpaces your ability to repay the loan; and (2) If you need five or six years to pay off your loan, you likely can't afford the vehicle. Make auto purchase decisions based on the *total* price paid, not the *monthly* payment.

- *Education loans* are one type of debt that has been historically considered "good debt," allowing students and their parents to believe that any amount of debt in pursuit of education is okay. But it's not. The "good" label on education loans has played a role in causing the outpaced inflation of the cost of higher education, which has risen at two and a half times the rate of inflation since 1985. Lifelong learning is priceless, but a college education isn't. Students should examine the value that education will provide relative to the expected salary after graduation. A good rule of thumb is to keep your aggregate school debt no higher than your expected first year's pay. We'll discuss this in greater detail in chapter 10 on education.

- *Home Equity Lines of Credit*, or HELOCs, are an interesting breed and can be used wisely or foolishly. It's an open line of credit secured by the homestead. This may surprise you: I believe that every homeowner who does not have a debt problem, but does have equity in their home, should have a HELOC. There are a few qualifications, though: (1) Don't pay closing costs, (2) Don't pay annual fees, (3) Avoid interest rates above the prime lending rate plus one percent, (4) Ensure that there is no pre-payment or early closing fees, and most importantly, (5) Don't use it!

Then why go through all the effort? Here's why: the last time you want to ask a bank for credit is when you need it. The HELOC should be used *only* in the case of true emergencies, when your emergency savings is exhausted, and for short-term liquidity. What qualifies as short-term liquidity? You're making an out-of-state move and you find the house of your dreams on a due-diligence trip, but the sale of your house hasn't yet closed. Use the HELOC to put the required deposit down and then pay it off completely after your house closes.

Please note that buying a car with a HELOC is almost never a good idea. Yes, the interest may be deductible, but if you don't aggressively pay off the loan, you'll be paying for your car for 20 years. Home improvements? Consider on a case-by-case basis, but please keep the total debt-to-equity ratio on the house under 90 percent.

• *Traditional mortgages* have to be "good debt," right? I've even heard of advisors and accountants saying, "You should have a mortgage—even in retirement—for the tax deduction." Hmm, let's explore this, shall we? Let's say you have a 5 percent mortgage rate, and you itemize your tax deductions and therefore are able to write off the interest (and only the interest) on your mortgage. If you're in a 25 percent tax bracket, this means that your effective mortgage rate is 3.75 percent. Yes, it's a low rate, but you're still paying interest. And only a portion of your mortgage payment goes to interest—the rest goes toward paying down your principal. You're in effect paying the bank a dollar to save a quarter.

Furthermore, the nature of mortgage amortization is that you pay a higher percentage of interest early in the mortgage and very little interest near the end. Therefore, if you have been paying on your mortgage for many years, you're not really deducting much interest anyway, virtually eliminating the mortgage interest deduction benefit.

All that said, there is no question that mortgage debt is better debt—perhaps even the "betterest." And for most of us, it's not an option if we want to own a home. But the only advisable mortgage in most cases is a traditional mortgage, where the home is paid off over 10, 15, 20, or 30 years. Most should stay away from anything exotic, like interest-only loans (which don't actually pay your house off), sub-prime mortgages (with high interest rates), "no-doc" loans (lovingly referred to as "liar loans"), or "option ARMs"[2] (where your debt may actually increase instead of decrease).

- What about reverse mortgages, the increasingly popular tool that allows homeowners with home equity to get money out of their house in retirement? I'd place them on the debt continuum between margin loans and auto loans. They are not to be confused with traditional mortgages.

  While their notoriously high fees have come down some, they pose an inherent problem—they increase your debt at a time when you'd prefer to eliminate it. I recommend that they be used only as a last resort, when a retiree intends to spend the remainder of her days (statistically) in her home and requires additional income.

Here's the bottom line on debt: Debt used wisely can help a household build wealth—today's modern definition of wealth, that is—when used to buy assets that appreciate in value. However, limiting debt—and eventually being debt free—grants uncommon peace of mind and is a key component of true wealth. Enough.

My advice is that you eliminate debt on the bad end of the spectrum as if it is financial enemy number one. Then, work to accelerate the repayment of better debt and plan to have all debt—including your mortgage—paid off by your expected retirement date.

So, what's the plan of attack on ridding yourself of the debt you already have?

Your Plan, Not Theirs

First, don't accept your creditor's plan for repayment. They make a living by putting you in debt and then stretching out the repayment period as long as possible. Let's look at a couple examples. First, a traditional mortgage, better debt example:

Let's say you take out a $350,000 mortgage at 5 percent for 30 years. In this example, the monthly payment (principal and interest only, not including taxes and insurance) would be $1,878.88. If you paid this every month for 30 years, you would pay a grand total of $676,395. That's $326,395 in interest.

But what if you paid this mortgage off in 20 years? Then, your monthly payment would be $2,309.85 per month, you'd pay $554,363 over the 20 years and $204,363 of that would be interest. By shortening the payback period, you'd save $122,032 in interest. That's not nothing.

"That sounds great," you say, "but it also means paying $431 more every month, and I can't handle that."

Fair enough, so let's take a look at simply increasing your monthly mortgage payment by $200—from $1,879 to $2,079. In this example, you'd cut 69 months off your mortgage, or almost six years. You'd spend a total of $254,989 on interest, still $71,406 less than in the case of the 30-year mortgage. And please don't forget the benefit of ridding yourself of a mortgage payment nearly six years sooner. Imagine the impact of that for a moment.

So, how do you turn your 30-year mortgage into 24 years and some change? Simple. Send your mortgage company two checks every month. You don't have to do it this way, but it's safer. Put "Principal Only" in the memo of the $200 check. Better yet, set them both up with online bill pay and watch 69 mortgage payments evaporate into thin air.

You can customize this to your situation. Just making one extra "Principal Only" mortgage payment each year results in a huge difference. Better yet, put those two extra paychecks to work if you get paid every other week instead of twice a month. Analyze your situation with the simple Bankrate Mortgage Loan Payoff Calculator.[3]

The mortgage pay-down analysis looks especially dramatic because we're using big numbers and long spans of time, but on a proportionate basis, RUC debt—really bad debt—looks even worse.

Consider for a moment that you have $15,000 in credit card debt, which, by the way, is just shy of the United States household average[4] as of December 2014. Let's imagine that the interest rate on your credit card is 20 percent (not uncommon) and that the default minimum payment required by the credit card company is the interest owed plus 1 percent of the balance (also not uncommon). In this example, your minimum payment would begin at $400 per month, but then the minimum payment goes down each month because of the way it is computed.

In this example, it would take 387 months—longer than a 30-year mortgage—to pay off this $15,000 credit card debt. The $15,000 would cost you a total of $39,392. That's $24,392 in interest alone. In the case of the 30-year mortgage at 5 percent, you were paying 1.92 times the amount borrowed; in the credit card case, you're paying a multiple of 2.63.

But what if you took control of this situation and created your own repayment schedule? For the very same card and interest rate, if you paid $500 per month, every month, you'd pay the $15,000 off in only 42 months expending only $5,967 in interest. Or, if you're able, switch to another card that offers a lower interest rate—say 10 percent instead of 20—and you'd pay the debt off in just under three years, losing a relatively paltry $2,333 to wealth-eating interest.

See how much interest you can kill with the Bankrate Credit Card Calculator.[5]

But what if there are multiple debts in your sights and you're trying to decide which to attack first?

Snowball Fight

It depends on who you want to lead the charge—the emotional Elephant or the rational Rider (chap. 3). If this debt issue is emotionally charged for you, and you've really struggled to get control of this in the past, Dave Ramsey's version of the debt snowball may be your best option.

Ramsey recommends you line your credit card debts up in order of balance size, with the smallest first, like this:

- $2,000 at 5 percent interest
- $5,000 at 22 percent interest
- $8,000 at 17.99 percent interest

He suggests paying the minimum on all three cards and then putting the extra money you'll make available toward the card with the *smallest balance* each month. The idea here is to get the snowball rolling emotionally—to give yourself an early victory in the battle against plastic. This Elephant-sensitive tactic helps many kick off their debt repayment, but as you may have guessed, this is not the ideal strategy from an economic perspective. You'll actually pay more in interest.

The problem with this method is that it ignores the Rider. I would prefer to see you engage the Rider as well, and pay as little interest to the banks as possible. Therefore, you would apply whatever extra monetary muscle you can muster each month to the card with the highest interest rate, like so:

- $5,000 at 22 percent interest
- $8,000 at 17.99 percent interest
- $2,000 at 5 percent interest

And, as you get that snowball rolling and improve your creditworthiness, you may even be able to accelerate the repayment by consolidating your balances to the lowest-rate card.

Turning the Tables

There is a way to turn the tables on the credit card companies. If—and only if—you have conquered any money disorders and rewritten your Money Scripts regarding debt dysfunction, then you may consider using a "rewards" credit card for all of your monthly purchases. As long as you pay off your balance every month, you'll pay no interest and likely thank the credit card company for contributing to your travel, lodging, or whatever other rewards you seek.

I, for one, am more than happy to fly my family home to visit relatives multiple times each year courtesy of my credit card company, and I don't think you should deprive yourself of the same, *as long as* you're not a debt dysfunction candidate.

Know Thyself

The one cash flow personality that we've not yet discussed is the Spendthrift, and I don't use this term casually. Unlike Spenders, whose tendencies are often rooted in the manageable self-deception of over-optimism, a true Spendthrift has a certifiable financial, and quite possibly psychological, disorder. The Spendthrift may be using poor spending habits—and almost certainly debt—to harm someone financially. They may seek to harm their spouse, children, or even themselves, consciously or subconsciously.

Sadly, while the Spendthrift is generally spurned by our culture, the other personality extreme—the Hoarder—is quite often admired for their frugality and material wealth. Sadder still, it is quite often the Hoarder who births the Spendthrift, proactively shaping the Money Scripts of loved ones by communicating in various ways that "Money is more important to me than you are."

So, let's be honest with ourselves. Where do you stand?

Where are *you*?

You're somewhere on the cash flow personality continuum, and knowing where you stand will help you take the next steps toward having Enough and sharing it with loved ones.

Simple Money Savings and Debt Summary

1. Savings and debt are opposite sides of the same coin. Having the former helps avoid the latter.

2. As we increase our cash reserves, we're able to buy ourselves degrees of financial independence, long before we're ready to retire.

3. Before you can get three, six, or twelve months of reserves saved, you've got to pass your first hurdle—getting one month's worth of living expenses. It's crucial to avoid living paycheck to paycheck.

4. The "good debt" and "bad debt" dichotomy is misleading. There is only bad debt and better debt.

5. The bottom line on debt: Debt used wisely can help a household build material wealth when used to purchase appreciating assets. But limiting debt—and eventually being debt free—grants an uncommon peace and is a key component of Enough.

What INSIGHTS and ACTIONS did you take from this chapter?

8

FINANCIAL STATEMENTS

Introducing Your New CFO

WHY do I need to read this chapter?

Every company has a CFO—the Chief Financial Officer—in charge of stewarding the firm's finances. Their job is to keep an eye on the company's assets, liabilities, and cash flow, and to report the state of the company's financial standing to the board.

How do you think the CFO would be received at the board meeting if, when asked to report, he said, "Ah, uh, well, money comes in, money goes out . . . it all seems to be working, uh, pretty well."

I think the CFO would likely be dusting off his résumé.

Well, guess who the de facto CFO is for you and your household?

That's right. It's you. And since you're also lead board member, I'm curious—how would you grade yourself as CFO?

Don't worry. If you didn't get rave reviews, I'll give you all the training you need in the next 10 minutes to make you a splendid new CFO of You, Inc. All you need to do is master three personal financial statements:

108

- Balance Sheet
- Cash Flow Statement
- Budget

In this chapter, we'll discuss the single most important indicator of a successful financial plan, your cash flow mechanism. Whether you make $10,000 or $10 million per year, it is your successful handling of cash flow that will be the driving force of any financial success, or failure.

So, how do you manage the flow of money into and out of your household? And more importantly, how do you intend to do so in the future?

Balance Sheet

The Balance Sheet takes a picture of your *present* financial situation. It lists your assets (the stuff you own) and liabilities (whatever you owe). Hopefully, when you subtract the latter from the former, the result is a positive number—your net worth, as in the example on the next page.

At its simplest, the overriding objective is to keep that net-worth number marching upward, with special attention paid to the items we highlighted in the Enough Index (chap. 6).

The Balance Sheet has a special influence due to the otherwise manic nature of the way we collect our most important financial information. Instead of separate statements strewn about for each checking, savings, mortgage, credit card, loan, brokerage, 401(k), IRA, and Roth IRA account, in the Balance Sheet we finally see everything in one place. Elegant simplicity.

You can access a Balance Sheet template like this at www.simple money.net/tools. This template is designed to emphasize elements that bump our Enough Index northward. I think it's important to update this document at least annually, but please know that it is possible to update *too* often. Because your assets invested in "the market" are in a constant state of flux, checking your balances too often can cause Enough-sapping anxiety. (Much more in chap. 9 on investing.)

Simple Money Balance Sheet

As of March 1, 2016

ASSETS

Real Estate

	Residence	$350,000
	Lake Lot	$15,000
Total Real Estate		**$365,000**

Emergency Reserves*

	Checking	$1,500
	Savings	$7,000
Total Emergency Reserves		**$8,500**

Retirement*

	401(k)s	$245,000
	Rollover IRAs	$125,000
	Roth IRAs	$25,000
Total Retirement		**$395,000**

Other Investments

	Vanguard	$14,000
	529 Education	$17,000
Total Other Investments		**$31,000**

TOTAL ASSETS	**$799,500**

LIABILITIES

Mortgages

	Residence Mortgage	$255,000
	Home Equity Line of Credit	$9,000
Total Mortgages		**$264,000**

RUC Debt*

	Visa	$3,000
	Best Buy	$730
Total RUC Debt		**$3,730**

Other Debt

	School Loan	$8,000
	Auto Loan	$7,000
Total Other Debt		**$15,000**

TOTAL LIABILITIES	**- $282,730**
NET WORTH	**$516,770**

*Enough Index Items

There are some excellent online tools and apps that will automate your balance sheet, but only as long as you have online access to your financial accounts and are willing to enter your usernames and passwords. Personal Capital and Mint are two tools I recommend. Personal Capital, in particular, offers a very sleek Net Worth feature that updates in real time.

Oh, and did I mention that both of these tools are free?

Cash Flow Statement

The Cash Flow Statement is an examination of our *past* spending, categorically. It's very difficult to project what we would like to spend in the future if we don't know what we've spent in the past. An example of a personal cash flow statement is shown on the next page.

As individuals, we tend to avoid cash flow analysis for some obvious reasons. For starters, it can be very tedious, especially if your household, like mine, is an active contributor to the nation's economic output. It's amazing how many and how various the transactions a family of four with a dog and turtle can produce. So, you have to set yourself up for success. If you try to review all of your household expenses on a monthly or quarterly basis, you'll almost certainly be overwhelmed by the scope of the project. If, however, you review your expenses weekly, it becomes a much more manageable task. Instead of feeling like getting a root canal, it's more like brushing your teeth. Tedious, yes, but manageable. The Rider can get bogged down by too much information, but he or she loves feeling in control.

The other big reason we avoid cash flow analysis is that it reminds us of how we fail. The Elephant hates feeling like a failure, and will therefore avoid opportunities to be reminded of such. I review our household spending weekly, and then in more detail at the end of the month. I don't know that we've ever had a month

Simple Money Cash Flow/Budget
For the Month of February 2016

INCOME	
Pre-Tax Savings*	
Jack	$840
Jill	$ -
HSA (Medical/Health)	$200
Total Pre-Tax Savings	**$1,040**
After-Tax Income	
Jack	$6,670
Jill	$3,000
TOTAL AFTER-TAX INCOME	**$9,670**

EXPENSES		
Fixed Expenses		
*Giving**	*$1,400*	
*Roth IRAs**	*$580*	
*Savings**	*$300*	
*RUC Debt**	*$300*	
Mortgage	$1,500	
School Loan	$50	
Auto Loan	$200	
Gym	$75	
Life Insurance	$60	
Disability Insurance	$50	
Auto Insurance	$130	
Tuition	$1,000	
Allowance	$100	
Total Fixed Expenses	**$5,745**	
Predictable Expenses		
Groceries	$1,000	
Utilities	$700	
Landscaping	$200	
Clothing	$150	
Gifts	$75	
Fuel	$200	
Auto Repair	$100	
Home	$60	
Vacation	$175	
Holidays	$150	
Total Predictable Expenses	**$2,810**	
Discretionary Expenses		
Jack	$110	
Jill	$110	
*Buffer**	*$200*	
Total Discretionary Expenses	**$420**	
TOTAL EXPENSES		**- $8,975**
SURPLUS or (DEFICIT)		**$695**

***Enough Index Items**

when we didn't overspend in some category. Fortunately, perfection is not the goal, and it helps to set the Elephant's expectations properly. Like baseball, cash flow analysis is an exercise in mistake management, not perfection.

Budget

We accommodate our imperfection by anticipating our inevitable failure in the form of budgeting. When I ask people, "Do you budget?" many of them say, "Yes, of course." If I probe further, I discover that what they call budgeting is merely tepid cash flow analysis. I'll hear, "Yes, when I pay my credit card bill, I glance down through my transactions."

Deliberate review of our past spending is the most time-intensive step in cash flow analysis, but it is in budgeting—forecasting a future spending plan—where we either succeed or fail.

"Shoot, we spent too much on groceries again last month" is a helpful observation only if you choose to spend less in the future or increase the grocery budget. Either one works, but it's your decision. That emphasis on choice is how Jesse Mecham, the creator of YNAB (YouNeedABudget.com) helps motivate his many followers. Here is the simple, but effective, four-step YNAB methodology:

1. Give every dollar a job.
2. Save for a rainy day.
3. Roll with the punches.
4. Live on last month's income.

"Where did all of my income go?" is an often-heard lament. It feels almost as if there's a force outside the household that gobbles up whatever excess cash exists. By giving every dollar a job, you'll know where it went, and thus have an opportunity to better direct it.

By saving for a rainy day, we do two things. We start by shielding ourselves from situations we'd label emergencies. But if that was its only purpose, Mecham could've just said, "Expect the unexpected." A rainy day fund can just as well be used to fund spontaneity.

Rolling with the punches helps to set our expectations properly. When we expect surprises as a matter of course, we don't freak out (as much) when they happen. We keep the Elephant from veering way off track. And when we live off of last month's income, we're no longer living paycheck to paycheck. This breathing room is the signature YNAB strategy, and it is an incredibly effective builder of Enough.

I asked Jesse Mecham, "So, what do you think about giving people guidance on how much they should spend in each category?" For example, here are some common rules of thumb you may have heard around the watercooler or from the preceding generations of your family:

- Spend no more than 25 percent of your net household income on housing, whether renting or owning.
- Spend no more than 15 percent on food.
- Limit entertainment spending to no more than 10 percent.
- Limit vacations to no more than 5 percent.
- Spend no more than 5 percent on auto loans.

In response, Mecham told me, "I honestly don't think those 'rules of thumb' are too useful. You move inland by 600 miles and everything changes." While he acknowledged that rules of thumb like this could be helpful either as starting points or for the purposes of refining objectives, every household is going to be different.

While it may be helpful to consider a host of different and thorough analytics that recommend certain allocations to various budgetary categories, the real reward in budgeting comes from tailoring a cash flow system to your own values and goals (chaps. 2 and 3).

Nudging Your Way to Financial Success

Economists Richard Thaler and Cass Sunstein coauthored the book *Nudge*, which has broad application for everything from international public policy to setting your monthly coffee budget. One of their more potent insights is that default options are incredibly powerful. When you crack open a new phone or computer, the setup process offers several opportunities for customization, but the path of least resistance is found in the default options. Not surprisingly, that's what most of us choose.

The most effective budgeters establish default options for themselves. If saving 10 percent and giving 10 percent are priorities, they simply default to living off 80 percent of their income. Everything else follows.

The power of setting defaults for household cash flow is strengthened even more by automating these defaults. You can automate more than you think—likely over 90 percent of your budget. Once you've automated as much of your budget defaults as possible, you can more freely enjoy spending whatever excess cash remains. Guilt free.

Consider the values-driven, goal-oriented, automated budget on the next page. Note that after funding your saving and giving priorities, your monthly expenses are broken down into Fixed Expenses—those that remain constant, like your mortgage and car payment; Predictable Expenses—those that tend to remain in a range, like groceries and utilities; and Discretionary Expenses, like money for eating out and going to the movies. It's your fun money. Of your entire budget, only your Discretionary Expenses can't be automated, and even then, you can purposefully decide to fund a budgetary category—or even a separate bank account—for fun money to ensure that you'll always have cash for spontaneity, a meaningful Enough boost.

What would your system look like?

Income

6% → 401(k)*

Most of your household budget can be automated

94%

Giving ← 10% — Checking

6% → Roth IRA

3% → Savings

75%

Fixed Expenses	Predictable Expenses	Discretionary Expenses
Mortgage	Groceries	Jack
School Loan	Utilities	Jill
Auto Loan	Landscaping	Joint
RUC Debt	Clothing	
Gym	Gifts	
Life Insurance	Fuel	
Disability Insurance	Auto Repair	
Auto Insurance	Home	
Tuition	Vacation	
Kids' Allowances	Holidays	
	Medical	

*Most 401(k) contributions will be pre-tax, but most other expenses will come out of after-tax earnings and may or may not be subject to tax deductibility.

How to Make Budgeting (Almost) Enjoyable

How might we view budgeting and cash flow differently, not as a tedious task that we *have* to do, but a life-giving task that we *get* to do? Not as a system of carrots and sticks that provoke rebellion, but a source of motivation? Not as a compulsion, but an impulsion? Let's recall Daniel Pink's successful motivational criteria from chapter 3. Then, budgeting would be

1. *Self-selected*: your initiative, not someone else's.
2. *Authentic*: consistent with your personal gifting and attributes.
3. *Others-oriented*: a cause that is bigger than you.

Budgeting can feel like a "should," but it doesn't have to. Do it on your terms. Here's what my self-selected routine looks like: After breakfast on Saturday morning, I top off my coffee, collect my wallet and the week's receipts from my wife, and head into my home office and close the door. I put on an album (collections of songs by a single artist, popular in the previous millennium) that I'm really enjoying and begin entering the week's purchases.

Yes, you heard me correctly. I actually review every receipt from every transaction in a given week and manually enter them into my budgeting software (more on that in a moment). Then I reconcile each transaction, toggling back and forth between the budgeting software and my bank's online list of transactions, just to make sure nothing slips between the cracks.

This is undeniable tedium, but for me, the weekly budget routine has almost become cathartic. Here's why:

It's easy. In fact, it's easy enough that I almost consider the budget element of this exercise to be ancillary. I'm enjoying a cup of coffee in solitude while soaking in some good music. Oh, I'm also doing the budget. Then, once I've completed the process, it's a big weight off my shoulders. I enjoy the rest of my weekend more, knowing where we stand financially.

Simple Money Journal Entry
Life-Giving Budgeting

I'm not suggesting you adopt my cash flow review routine, although you're welcome to. Instead, what would a life-giving budgeting exercise look like for you?

The Freedom of Discipline

Does the word *discipline* have a positive or negative connotation for you? I think for most of us, our foremost gut reaction is negative. It feels restrictive. It feels like an imposition, stealing our freedom. But, when rightly applied, discipline actually breeds freedom.

How? Well, consider a single line-item in our household budget: "Date Night." There are many joys that come from being a parent with young kids, but the demands of such a household have a tendency to relegate Mom and Dad's relationship to being more about business than romance. That's what date night is for, to remind us what got this whole family thing started.

It's hard enough to muster the requisite creative energy to plan a date night, from lining up a babysitter to making dinner reservations and checking movie times. And that doesn't even take into consideration what goes into planning those special occasions. Then you have to worry about whether or not you have the money, 'cause a great date night ain't cheap if you do it right.

For many years, we didn't have a specific category within our budget to fund this marriage-strengthening exercise. So it always felt like we were stealing from another category to raise the cash necessary to fund our night on the town. This was no doubt the last straw, and it led to the abandonment of many date night plans. But now it's funded. Money is set aside each month to ensure we don't have to hurt ourselves financially to help our marriage.

The "restriction" of tracking our cash flow surprisingly breeds the opportunity for spontaneity where it might otherwise have been impossible. Or, as Richard Foster, author of *Celebration of Discipline*, puts it, "Discipline brings freedom."

Sounds great, right? So, how do you get started if you don't have a budget?

Cash Flow Tools

There are many online tools and apps available to help make budgeting as easy and effective as possible. Most of them are variations on the theme of envelope budgeting. With the original envelope system, you cash your paycheck and put predetermined amounts of cash in envelopes marked with the budget category. Then, when you get to the bottom of the cash in each category, you're done.

The envelope system certainly works, and its tangible nature helps get more of our senses involved. It is, however, cumbersome and less than secure with all that cash floating around. It should be used primarily as a short-term boot camp for jump-starting a budgeting initiative. You may consider going straight to an online- or software-based system instead.

I believe the easiest system to use is Mint.com, which I mentioned previously. Their system will actually aid you in more deeply understanding the process of establishing and maintaining your budget. Furthermore, if you're willing to plug your online bank usernames and passwords into the system, it will practically do your budgeting for you. It automatically categorizes each transaction and lets you know when your budget limit is approaching.

Newer entrants to the high-tech money management space, like Levelmoney and Personal Capital, are compelling and surprisingly easy to use. But can budgeting be too easy?

I asked Jesse Mecham, the founder of YNAB cash flow software, why he hasn't added the Mint-like features of auto-categorization to his well-respected program. He told me that, while convenient, the auto-categorization makes the process *too* easy. "I didn't know there was such a thing," I said. But his response made a lot of sense.

If the program is too automated, Jesse told me, then budgeters aren't cognizant enough of their spending and the impact of individual transactions. I buy that. Cash flow management is most effective as an exercise in deliberate self-awareness.

YNAB involves a bit steeper learning curve than Mint, and it does have a price tag.[1] But it offers sufficient instructions and online classes to make it worth every penny.

Of course, it's important to remember that cash flow management is just a means to an end, a tool to be used in navigating the three guarantees in financial planning—surprises, change, and failure.

Three Guarantees in Financial Planning

We err if we believe adequate preparation will help us avoid *surprises* in life. Preparation simply lessens the potentially negative impact of those surprises. The antidote for surprises is *margin*.

Margin is the buffer between what we think will happen and what actually does. Humans are notorious for underestimating life's hurdles and overestimating our abilities to overcome them. This is why it takes 50 percent longer to finish your paper, why it costs 25 percent more to complete your home renovation, and why I should leave 10 minutes earlier every time I'm driving somewhere.

There are a few ways we can employ margin to better navigate life's financial surprises. The first is to maintain sufficient emergency reserves, discussed at length in the previous chapter. The second is to set each of our budget categories just a shade above our average spending, like setting your watch five minutes fast. And finally, fund a separate budget line item that reads "Margin" or "Buffer," just to soak up any monthly overspending.

Margin serves us well both in money and life. Overcommitment is the scourge of our generation; busyness is the tarnished badge of honor we wear to validate our self-worth. But it's not Enough.

The second guarantee is *change*. It's been said that death and taxes are life's only two guarantees, but taxes appear optional in several European countries and I'm still hoping to go out like the prophet Elijah, on a chariot of fire. Change, however, is inescapable and shouldn't come as a surprise. The counteragent to this guarantee is *flexibility*.

From a cash flow perspective, flexibility is especially valuable when we change jobs or homes. You might move to an area with higher taxes and be forced to endure a reduction in your net pay, which affects all your budget categories. Even a change as apparently innocuous as your employer making the switch from paying you twice a month to biweekly can have a meaningful impact on your budget. And that's not even to mention a job change with a totally new compensation regime. A planned pregnancy is no surprise, but it will impact your budget materially the next couple of decades (at least).

It helps to hold very little sacred in your cash flow planning, as any number of life's changes—welcome or unwelcome—can force you to bend your expectations and planning. And remember, that which is unwilling to bend often breaks.

The last guarantee in financial planning sounds a bit defeatist. However, *failure* need not be viewed as terminal. Have you heard the term "going to failure" in the context of fitness and exercise? The idea is that our muscles grow when we allow them to be expended to the point of exhaustion. We must push beyond our limitations to grow, even though we know that the immediate result will be failure.

That we have an opportunity to grow through failure doesn't mean it's painless. It hurts, but the pain is salved by *grace*, something we must often extend to ourselves and anyone we're partnered with financially. Grace is unearned favor—it's a slate cleaning. It's erasing the record of wrongs, allowing us to move forward with dignity and the confidence that we can do better.

In the words of philosopher (and Pearl Jam frontman) Eddie Vedder, "[It] makes much more sense to live in the present tense."

Matrimony and Money

With more than 50 percent of marriages ending in divorce and more than 50 percent of those splits attributed to financial disagreements, it's safe to say that money is the most dangerous element within the context of matrimony. My wife and I are no different. Our cash flow personalities are markedly different, attributes we can clearly trace to how we were raised.

My father was the first of his lineal descendants to go to college, an endeavor he took on without any financial aid from his family. They simply couldn't afford it. His father, a World War II vet, was stably employed but in a trade that didn't allow for any extravagance at home.

Dad got a degree in engineering, only compounding the effect of his frugal upbringing. (Know any engineers? You understand what I'm talking about.) It became part of his parental duty to ensure that my brothers and I were not prone to indulgence. Even though we were far better off financially than he in his upbringing, my father believed that familiarity with deprivation was a useful tool in developing financial discipline. So, you can guess what his response was when I pleaded to get the sleek Adidas Samba soccer shoes because "All the cool kids have them!" You guessed it—Keds.

My wife's father was born into abject poverty, in a German work camp at the tail end of World War II after his parents' homeland, the Ukraine, had been taken over. His family was blessed to immigrate to Canada, but beginning from scratch without any marketable skills, life in Calgary was bare bones.

After putting himself through undergraduate and medical school, which eventually afforded him a much more comfortable living than the one he'd known as a child, my father-in-law made it his mission to ensure his children would not feel the sense of desperation he knew so well.

Even though both of our fathers grew up relatively poor, they each employed what they learned honorably—but very differently—as parents. How do you think all this disparate background played out in the early years of our marriage?

On paper, Andrea and I don't represent polar extremes. She's not a consummate Spender and I'm not a dedicated Saver (chap. 7). But it sure as heck feels like we're opposites sometimes. We're not the only couple to amplify each other's less-than-admirable financial characteristics, are we? The statistics would suggest not.

So, how do we keep our financial dissonance from becoming a fatal flaw in our marriage? First, we try to see each other not as a stingy scrooge and a wasteful spendthrift but as a collection of our life experiences. As Rick Kahler, the Money Script guy, says, "All financial behaviors, no matter how illogical, make perfect sense when we understand the underlying beliefs about money."[2] These are informed by our life experiences, especially those of our youth (chap. 2).

Next, we stop demonizing each other and try to see ourselves as closer to one another on the continuum. And best of all, we try to recognize the strengths of the other as complements to our weaknesses, not as threats.

This is, of course, easier said than done—especially in the heat of disagreement—but it could just save your marriage.

Simple Money Journal Entry

If you're married, how well do you understand your spouse's—and your own—financial past and the impact it has on the present?

Congratulations!

You've done the challenging but rewarding work of the five foundational chapters. You also know where you are on the map financially and you've taken stock of your cash flow personality strengths and weakness on your way to accepting your new role as an effective CFO for your household.

Now it's time to start planning for your future, beginning with a look at the simple investment portfolio that has beaten the pros.

Simple Money Financial Statements Summary

1. You are your household's default CFO—how are you doing?

2. The most important indicator of a successful financial plan is the household cash flow mechanism.

3. There are three personal financial statements we use to navigate our financial realm:

   - *The Balance Sheet* takes a picture of your present financial situation.

   - *The Cash Flow Statement* examines our categorical past spending.

   - *The Budget* forecasts a spending plan for our near future.

4. Cash flow management, even with the best tools available, isn't going to be fun, but we can design a rhythm that is self-selected, authentic, and others-oriented to help motivate ourselves to action.

5. The three guarantees in personal finance are surprises, change, and failure, but they can be countered with margin, flexibility, and grace.

What INSIGHTS and ACTIONS
did you take from this chapter?

PART 3

PLANNING FOR THE INEVITABLE

*Planning for the future is made simpler
by bringing it into the present.*

9

INVESTING

A Simple Portfolio That's Beaten the Pros

WHY do I need to read this chapter?

More information is available today than at any time in history. Especially regarding investing, most of the information available is conflicting. This makes sense because each of the world's financial superpowers, gurus, newsletters, authors, and bloggers rely on differentiation to sell their philosophies.

Whose philosophy can and can't be relied upon? The good news is that you can ignore most of what is already out there. Instead of relying on the opinion of a "guru" or the predictions of a prophet, you can choose to rely on the evidence—the peer-reviewed, back-tested, academically vetted, reputably published findings.

While you can't guarantee the future, you can build a surprisingly simple portfolio that has consistently outperformed the majority of professional investors in the past.

The *Simple Money Portfolio*—engineered for Enough (chap. 1) and designed with both the Elephant and Rider (chap. 3) in mind—is on the other side of a mountain of complexity. I won't torture you with all of the evidence that goes into this strategy, but it's important you know enough to maintain a conviction to stick with whatever strategy you choose to employ. So please allow me to establish some context as we work our way toward your portfolio prescription.

A Compressed History of "the Market"

Since 1926, the annualized rate of return of the US stock market has been approximately 10 percent per year. If you invested $10,000 in the US stock market in 1926 and "let it ride," you'd have roughly $40 million to show for it today, 87 years later. Not bad.

Simple Definitions

Annualized rate of return: When an investment period is more or less than one year, an annualized return shows what you would have earned per year.

But oh, how it would've been a bumpy ride. You'd have lost 90 percent—yes, nine-zero—of your investment following the 1929 crash, and it wouldn't have been until 1943 that you'd get back to where you started prior to the Great Depression. From 1949 through 1966, the market experienced consistent growth, but from the mid-sixties through 1981, the market traversed 15 years of relative mediocrity. In 1982, however, a bull market began that, despite numerous short-term scares, wouldn't be reversed until the turn of the century. Fourteen years later, we're looking back on another decade-plus stretch of relatively paltry market returns. Do the phrases "tech bubble" or "financial crisis" ring any bells?

Bull markets, by the way, are good. Bear markets are bad. If you're looking for a way to remember that, bulls thrust their horns upward, the direction we'd prefer to see the stock market go. Bears use their powerful paws to thrash downward on their victims.

Do You Have What It Takes?

Let's leave the realm of hypothetical percentages for a moment and put you in the position of many who experienced the real-life pain of market ups and downs. We'll determine if you have what it takes to endure the white-knuckle roller coaster ride of the market.

You decided to retire at the end of 2007. You sold your house and downsized, netting an additional $250,000 to add to your $750,000 retirement nest egg, bringing your total retirement savings to $1 million. The income from your nest egg will supplement your Social Security retirement benefit and a small pension. (More on both of those in chap. 11.)

The market had always treated you pretty well, and you'd recovered nicely from the bursting of the tech bubble in the early 2000s. You were confident enough in the market that you left all of your money in a handful of brand-name mutual funds that owned mostly large company stocks. You were certain that you'd be able to ride out any downside. Then came 2008.

In a single year, you saw the head and shoulders of your million-dollar nest egg lopped off—losing $370,000. But the slide didn't stop there. With optimism brewing over the holidays, you waited to see what happened in the beginning of 2009. What happened was that you lost even more. But you were also taking the old standard of 5 percent per year income stream out of your original portfolio to live on in retirement, so by the end of March 2009, you had only about half of your $1 million nest egg left.

Do you have what it takes?

The Downside of Downside

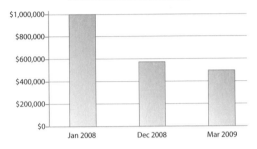

What did you do next?

The Behavior Gap

You sold, of course, right as the market began its recovery and "refunded" your losses. The emotional Elephant took over and tossed the rational Rider (chap. 3).

There's no shame in this. It felt like the rational thing to do, especially because, at that time, even the world's top economic and investment minds acknowledged that the crisis could have deepened to Depression-like levels.

But you acted on the basis of the limited information at hand and the emotional turmoil within. Carl Richards, author and *New York Times* contributor, coined a term for this persistent investment error: the "behavior gap."

It's the gap between the return that invest*ments* produce and the return that invest*ors* in those investments actually earn. They are the same only if an investor holds the investment the entire period in question. As you might suspect, many investors earn less than the very mutual funds in which they invest *because they don't remain invested*, getting in and out at the behest of their emotions.

We have a tendency to wait until everyone, including our barista, is blabbing about how much money they've made in the market before we finally decide to get in. That inevitably seems to occur near the market's top. Then, like our friend who retired at the perfectly wrong time, investors historically wait until the market has sufficiently bruised and bloodied them before giving up and getting out.

In short, the research has proven that the average investor has an uncanny propensity to buy high and sell low, the opposite of the profitable investing maxim. As Benjamin Graham, the father of value investing and Warren Buffett's mentor, said, "The investor's chief problem—and even his worst enemy—is likely to be himself."

Are investors their own worst enemies?

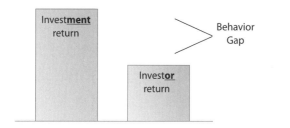

There's got to be a better way forward. One better than simply relying on the past to repeat itself and then the second time around knowing enough to talk yourself out of hitting the eject button, right? Can we create an investment plan that accommodates both the Elephant and the Rider?

Thankfully, yes.

The Real Point of Investing

The real point of investing is *not* actually to make money but to have a better life and facilitate Enough (chap. 1).

The primary objective of investing in stocks, however, *is* to make money. The primary objective of investing in bonds and cash, then, is to help you stay invested in stocks when it inevitably becomes difficult to do so. The net effect should be that investing adds value to your life, in accordance with your priorities (chap. 2) and in pursuit of your goals (chap. 3).

Evidence-based investing forces us to submit all our opinions and educated guesses to actual peer-reviewed scrutiny. The evidence shows, after all, that it is extremely difficult to "beat the market." There is a significant body of research, however, that indicates certain asset classes—slices of the full market spectrum—have performed better than others. For example, you already likely know that stocks have historically performed better than bonds. What you may not know is that small-company stocks have outperformed large-company stocks, and value stocks historically have outperformed growth stocks.

Simple Definitions

- **Stocks**—Shares of partial ownership in a company.
- **Bonds**—Loans to a company that pay interest.
- **"The market"**—Typically refers to a selection of the largest United States companies, best represented by the S&P 500 Index.
- **Index**—A tracking mechanism for various asset classes.
- **Asset Class**—A collection of investments with similar characteristics; could be as broad as "stocks" and "bonds" or as specific as "Japanese small cap value."

Unfortunately, the asset classes that have historically produced outsized returns have also required more intestinal fortitude, at times, in order to reap a reward. Their highs may be higher, but their lows can also be lower. What's more, they tend to perform poorly in the scariest of times.

Distinct Asset Classes Provide Distinct Return Profiles

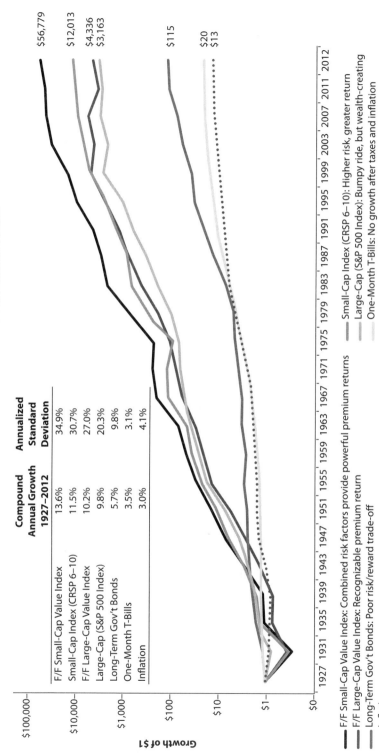

	Compound Annual Growth 1927–2012	Annualized Standard Deviation
F/F Small-Cap Value Index	13.6%	34.9%
Small-Cap Index (CRSP 6–10)	11.5%	30.7%
F/F Large-Cap Value Index	10.2%	27.0%
Large-Cap (S&P 500 Index)	9.8%	20.3%
Long-Term Gov't Bonds	5.7%	9.8%
One-Month T-Bills	3.5%	3.1%
Inflation	3.0%	4.1%

Growth of $1

$100,000 — $56,779

$10,000 — $12,013
$4,336
$3,163

$1,000 —

$115

$100 —

$20
$13

$10 —

$1 —

$0 —

1927 1931 1935 1939 1943 1947 1951 1955 1959 1963 1967 1971 1975 1979 1983 1987 1991 1995 1999 2003 2007 2011 2012

— F/F Small-Cap Value Index: Combined risk factors provide powerful premium returns
— F/F Large-Cap Value Index: Recognizable premium return
— Long-Term Gov't Bonds: Poor risk/reward trade-off
····· Inflation

— Small-Cap Index (CRSP 6–10): Higher risk, greater return
— Large-Cap (S&P 500 Index): Bumpy ride, but wealth-creating
— One-Month T-Bills: No growth after taxes and inflation

Data supplied by Dimensional Fund Advisors. Indices are not available for direct investment. Their performance does not reflect the expenses associated with the management of an actual portfolio nor do indices represent results of actual trading. Information from sources deemed reliable, but its accuracy cannot be guaranteed. Performance is historical and does not guarantee future results. Total returns includes reinvestment of dividends. Source: Dimensional Fund Advisors.

The Evolution of Evidence-Based Investing in Four Steps

Fortunately, "the market" so commonly referred to in the financial media isn't the only market. So let's examine the impact of blending other asset classes—like bonds, the stocks of smaller companies, and the stocks of international companies—with our large company United States stock market exposure. This is a story first told to me by Larry Swedroe, a chief proponent of evidence-based investing and the author of numerous books on the subject, including his most recent, *The Incredible Shrinking Alpha*, coauthored with Andrew Berkin.

To ensure we're comparing apples to apples, we'll conduct our portfolio examination over the past thirty-nine years, for which there is accurate data across a broad range of asset classes. Since 1975, we have experienced some of the market's most pronounced ups and downs, but the market has survived them quite respectably. The S&P 500—likely the best United States market-tracking device, which mimics the aggregate price movement of 500 influential stocks—has had an annualized return of 12.15 percent.

Throughout that time, however, there was a great deal of market volatility—that is, the dispersion of market returns was wide. The market suffered three straight down years for the first time since the Great Depression beginning in 2000, and in 2008, I don't need to remind you that the market got hammered. That year, the S&P 500 lost 37 percent. Its best year during that stretch came in 1995, when the market was up 37 percent.

We measure the volatility of a particular investment by examining its standard deviation. It's a proportionate gauge of how far the actual returns of an investment deviate from its average return. Between 1975 and 2013, the standard deviation of the S&P 500 was 16.9 percent, which won't mean a whole lot until we compare it to the standard deviation of a portfolio that includes other asset classes.

1975–2013	Annualized Return	Annual Standard Deviation
S&P 500	12.15%	16.98%

To do so, we'll look through the lens of the Fama/French "Three-Factor Model," proposed by Nobel Prize winners Kenneth French and Eugene Fama. At its simplest, the Three-Factor Model recognizes a triad of persistent investing factors that tend to offer investors a "premium" in the form of higher returns. The first factor recognizes the higher returns expected for investing in stocks over bonds, but it also forces us to acknowledge that if we want a chance at a higher return, we'll need to accept greater risk and increased volatility. If we, however, blend a helping of stock exposure along with conservative bonds (note the addition of 5-Year Treasuries), the overall portfolio volatility goes down dramatically, as evidenced in the portfolio below:

Step 1: Add Fixed Income to Stabilize

Portfolio 1
S&P 500 Index   60%
5-Year Treasuries   *40%*

1975–2013	Annualized Return	Annual Standard Deviation
S&P 500	12.15%	16.98%
Portfolio 1	10.80%	10.60%

The expected return drops by a relative 11 percent (an absolute 1.35 percentage points), a sacrifice most would be willing to make, especially when the volatility is 38 percent lower!

The benefits of stability in a portfolio cannot be underestimated because the evidence, now termed the *endowment effect*, suggests that portfolio declines are twice as painful to investors as portfolio gains are blissful. This helps explain the behavior gap and screams that the average investor should help keep himself in the game by reducing the downside risk through a meaningful allocation to conservative fixed income.

You need to construct a portfolio that you can live with long term, and I recommend that you err on the side of conservatism, because you don't know exactly how you'll respond to sharp market downside until you get there.

Since the foremost portfolio stabilizing agent is fixed income, and since the primary reason we hold fixed income is to steady our portfolio in bad times to avoid exceeding our risk tolerance, it only makes sense to hold the most stable of the stable investments. Those include FDIC-insured CDs, US Treasuries, agencies, and only if you're in a high tax bracket, AAA- and AA-rated diversified municipal bonds. These can be either general obligation bonds or essential service revenue bonds.

Yes, I omitted corporate bonds from that list as well as high-yield "junk" bonds, because these varietals tend to exhibit more stock-like risk characteristics in down markets. If you're going to take more risk, you may as well do it in the asset class that offers a higher potential reward—stocks. (While the annual premium for taking stock risk has been about 8 percent, the annual risk premium for taking corporate credit risk has been only about 0.3 percent.)

The second of Fama and French's three factors is size. Popular culture's mantra of "bigger is better" does not apply here. In this case small companies outperformed their larger cohorts by a noticeable margin. Thus, splitting one's stock exposure between large company stocks and small company stocks results in a meaningful increase in the portfolio's return, but also (to a lesser degree) in its standard deviation:

Step 2: Add Small Cap Stocks

Portfolio 2

S&P 500 Index	30%
Fama/French US Small Cap Index	30%
5-Year Treasuries	40%

1975–2013	Annualized Return	Annual Standard Deviation
S&P 500	12.15%	16.98%
Portfolio 1	10.80%	10.60%
Portfolio 2	12.00%	11.20%

Factor number three is value. Fama and French demonstrated that, over a long time horizon, *value stocks* (companies whose share price is low relative to their intrinsic value) have a higher expected return than *growth stocks* (like social media stocks that haven't made a profit yet). Adding them increases the portfolio's expected rate of return, while also increasing its volatility. Take a look:

Step 3: Add Value Stocks

Portfolio 3

S&P 500 Index	15%
Fama/French US Large Value	*15%*
Fama/French US Small Cap Index	15%
Fama/French US Small Value	*15%*
5-Year Treasuries	40%

1975–2013	Annualized Return	Annual Standard Deviation
S&P 500	12.15%	16.98%
Portfolio 1	10.80%	10.60%
Portfolio 2	12.00%	11.20%
Portfolio 3	12.50%	12.30%

But here's where it gets really interesting. Another Nobel Prize–winning brainiac, Harry Markowitz, shocked the world—the investing world, anyway—when he showed that you can stir a *more volatile* asset class into the mix and actually see the overall portfolio volatility go *down*. Case in point:

Step 4: Add International Stocks

Portfolio 4

S&P 500 Index	7.5%
Fama/French US Large Value	7.5%
Fama/French US Small Cap Index	7.5%
Fama/French US Small Value	7.5%
MSCI EAFE Value Index	*15%*
Dimensional Int'l Small Cap	*15%*
5-Year Treasuries	40%

1975–2013	Annualized Return	Annual Standard Deviation
S&P 500	12.15%	16.98%
Portfolio 1	10.80%	10.60%
Portfolio 2	12.00%	11.20%
Portfolio 3	12.50%	12.30%
Portfolio 4	12.50%	11.50%

In this particular case, we reduced the portfolio's United States stock exposure and introduced exposure to international stocks. While they are a more volatile asset class, the total portfolio's volatility is actually reduced. The reason is because the asset classes are not highly correlated. That means, at times, there is a divergence between how the two asset classes respond to the same market and economic stimuli.

But here's something you may not have noticed along our four-step portfolio construction journey: By the time we get to Step 4, we have constructed a portfolio with a higher expected rate of return than "the market" with substantially less volatility. Who wouldn't want that?

The success of the portfolio isn't based on constantly jumping in and out of the market or betting on hot stock tips and rock-star mutual fund managers. Its success comes from evidence-based diversification and discipline.

The Simple Money Portfolio

Our four-step process brings us to the Simple Money Portfolio. It's a moderate portfolio grounded in decades of academically scrutinized, peer-reviewed research into the "science" of investing. Between 1975 and 2013, it managed a *higher* annualized return than "the market," and did so taking meaningfully *less* risk:

The Simple Money Portfolio

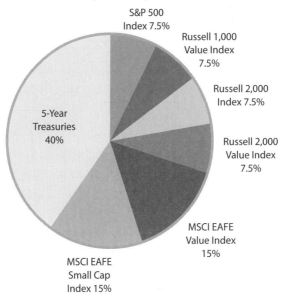

How, you might ask, can a simple, index-based portfolio outperform the market and most professional investors while taking less risk?

- It diversifies the stock-based investments across a broad range of asset classes that historically have rewarded investors with higher returns than the broader market (small cap stocks and value stocks).

- It diversifies half of the stock exposure beyond the United States and Canada into the international landscape. This exposes the portfolio to many opportunities beyond our borders. But because foreign stocks often don't move in concert with domestic stocks, investing in these riskier stocks actually reduces the overall risk of the portfolio.

- It lowers the overall risk by investing 40 percent of the portfolio in fixed-income instruments, like bonds. While some will decry the Simple Money Portfolio for being too conservative, the research clearly demonstrates that most investors aren't capable of enduring the volatility inherent in riskier portfolios. The best portfolio strategy is the one you can live with.

- It limits the negative impact of riskier fixed-income securities by investing in only the most conservative bonds (or bond equivalents) available.

Although it's surprisingly simple, there is a ton of intellectual horsepower under the hood. It is engineered to forestall the emotions of fear and greed that get the Elephant in trouble, and the Rider appreciates its systematic approach to investing.

Although it may not be the perfect portfolio for you, it could be. Your ideal portfolio will account, most importantly, for your ability, willingness, and need to take risk, reshaping your portfolio by adjusting for those factors. (Go through an exercise designed for this purpose at www.simplemoneyportfolio.com/customize.) And it's vastly better than inaction, investing without a strategy, or chasing a poorly conceived strategy.

Why haven't you heard of it before? Well, it has earned the disdain of the broader financial industry because it's beaten most of their high-paid stock-and-bond-picking pros. They're too busy trying to beat the market, or at least convincing us that it's possible.

But Why Not Try to "Beat the Market"?

But why settle? Why not actively work to beat the benchmarks instead of maintaining a more passive, disciplined approach? In short, it's because the probability of beating the market is so low that it's prohibitive to try.

First, we must define what it means to actually "beat the market." We're not talking about simply outperforming one of the major stock or bond market indexes, like the S&P 500 or the Barclays US Aggregate Bond indexes.

Investors who take more risk than these benchmarks contain in years where taking risk is rewarded could—even should—have a higher expected rate of return. But doing so does not equate to a feat of investing brilliance. No, in order to claim dominance over the market, an investor must achieve a higher *risk-adjusted* rate of return—the prized, yet elusive, Alpha.

Beta, in investing parlance, is a risk measurement of the overall market. The market has a default Beta of 1. An investment with a Beta of 1.5, therefore, is taking on more risk than the market and should enjoy a proportionately higher reward at a time when the market has an upward trajectory. Of course, you should also expect to lose more on the downside. An investment with a Beta of less than 1 should respond to market stimuli with less gusto, or volatility, than the market.

Beta is all around us, but Alpha is more like a shrouded ghost that investors occasionally glimpse but rarely capture.

Depending on the year, you'll find statistics confirming that the majority of actively managed funds—mutual funds and hedge funds, whose very existence is justified only by the unlikely hope of attaining Alpha—underperform their appropriate benchmarks. In any typical year, about 60 percent of actively managed funds underperform, and the figure increases as the horizon lengthens.

An even more colossal failing is active managers' inability to beat the market over an extended period of time, or even a few years consecutively. A Vanguard study confirming previous research found that only 18 percent of active managers were able to outperform their benchmark over the fifteen-year period from 1998 through 2012.[1] And that's before taxes, which are often the largest expense of actively managed funds.

Fully 97 percent of active funds underperformed in at least five of those years, and "two-thirds of them experienced at least three *consecutive* years of underperformance"during that span.[2]

Moneyball

Perhaps you've seen the movie *Moneyball* or read the book by Michael Lewis upon which the film was based. It's an underdog story about how a financially underresourced baseball team, the Oakland Athletics, managed to compete with and often beat the richest teams in the league. They did so by applying a systematic, evidence-based approach to the recruitment of team talent. Stripping themselves of the predominant prejudices of the sport—for example, that ranked players whose visible physiques mirrored the athletic ideal higher—they focused entirely on the evidence before them, favoring calculations like on-base percentage.

The subtitle of *Moneyball* is "The Art of Winning an Unfair Game." According to many, investing is an unfair game, dominated by Wall Street's power brokers who operate primarily in pursuit of personal gain. (Incidentally, Michael Lewis, a former Salomon Brothers bond trader, is one who holds this opinion.)

But much in the same way that the evidence helped the A's compete with baseball's most powerful franchises, evidenced-based investing can help you compete with—and often beat—Wall Street at its own game.

Simple Money Investing Summary

1. Instead of relying on the opinion of a guru or the predictions of a prophet, you can choose to rely on the evidence—the peer-reviewed, back-tested, academically vetted, reputably published evidence.

2. If you invested $10,000 in the United States stock market in 1926 and "let it ride," you'd have roughly $40 million to show for it today, but it was an almost unendurable ride—including a 90 percent loss following the 1929 crash. There's got to be a better way than simply buying and holding "the market." (And there is.)

3. The emotional damage done by market downside leads to the "behavior gap," causing investors to jump in and out of investments, inevitably earning less than the investments they hold.

4. The real point of investing is *not* to actually make money but to have a better life. The primary objective of investing in stocks, however, *is* to make money. The primary objective of investing in bonds and cash, then, is to help you stay invested in stocks when it becomes difficult to do so.

5. The evidence suggests the following:
   - It's extremely difficult to "beat the market" by picking stocks.
   - Stocks have historically performed better than bonds.
   - Small-company stocks have outperformed large-company stocks.
   - Value stocks have outperformed growth stocks.

6. The *Simple Money Portfolio*—broadly diversified with 40 percent in bonds and tilted in the direction of outperforming asset classes—has had returns as good or better than "the market" since 1975, and has done so with meaningfully less risk.

7. Much in the same way that Billy Beane helped the Oakland Athletics beat "superior" teams with evidence-based baseball, evidence-based investing can help you compete with—and often beat—Wall Street at its own game.

What INSIGHTS and ACTIONS did you take from this chapter?

10

EDUCATION

Getting Schooled

WHY do I need to read this chapter?

Knowledge is vital. It's the wellspring of so many of life's blessings. Getting an education, however, is a value proposition. Lifelong learning may be priceless, but a college education is not. Indeed, it can come with a hefty price tag.

The proliferation of student loans, and the presupposition that they are "good debt" (chap. 7), has converged with the perception that obtaining a college degree is a mandatory milestone. The collision of these factors has created what some are describing as an education bubble.

But whether you are a parent supporting a student or a student yourself, please know that while education can indeed be very expensive, it is possible to get a rich educational experience that is surprisingly inexpensive. In this chapter, we'll discuss how. We'll also give educational benefactors—generally parents and grandparents—some guidance with the Non-Conformist's Four-Step Education Savings Plan.

Offending NYU

In May 2012, I had the distinct privilege of being interviewed by David Greene on NPR's *Morning Edition*.[1] We were discussing education and, in particular, its cost and the detrimental effects of burdensome student loans in a slow job market. I insisted that we must view education as a value proposition. We should consider what we'll get out of our time at college before committing to the cost, and especially before undertaking any debt to pay for it.

"You need to gauge how much you're willing to pay for your education based on how much money it's going to help you make in the future," I posited.

I then launched into a hypothetical example. "When I'm talking to a student who might be passionately interested in social work, I'm going to recommend that they not necessarily consider going to NYU and racking up a ton of bills that they will not be able to pay back."

I have several good friends in the crucial field of social work, and I know they are sorely underpaid. And while I could have used any pricey, prestigious university in my example, for whatever reason, I pulled New York University out of thin air. At the time, I didn't even know for sure if they had a school of social work. I'd soon find out.

I got a two-page letter coauthored by the dean of the NYU Silver School of Social Work and the president of the National Association of Social Workers, both of whom were also professors at NYU. First, they had misconstrued my mention of social work as a slight to the profession. Then, they endeavored to convince me of the value of NYU's diploma in social work, as indicated by their high standings in the oft-cited *U.S. News and World Report* rankings.

In my response, I assured them that my mention of social work was no accident, and especially, no disparagement. Then I got to the value proposition. I'd researched their ranking of social work schools in *U.S. News*. Indeed, NYU landed at a respectable #16. But it was tied, and guess with what school? My home state's (public) University of Maryland, Baltimore.

"How then, as a financial planner," I queried, "could I rationally recommend that a prospective student pay double or triple the cost for a similarly ranked education, especially if they are using debt to pay for school?"

Needless to say, I didn't get a reply.

A Look at the Numbers

While few would disagree with me that price should be a consideration when making educational decisions, it's not reflected in our behavior. An undergraduate degree is now widely considered "the thirteenth grade," a requisite step for anyone hoping to be successful in life. The cost of an education, therefore, reflects this increased demand.

"Since 1985, the overall consumer price index," which is the primary measure of inflation, "has risen 115 percent while the college education inflation rate has risen nearly 500 percent," said Steve Odland in a 2012 *Forbes* article.[2]

And while the past few years have seen the gap between overall inflation and the cost of college draw closer, education is still outpacing inflation, according to Bloomberg. "Including room and board, costs average $18,943 for in-state students at public schools and $32,762 for out-of state residents. At private schools, the bill is $42,419."[3] Per year.

Those numbers are averages, of course. If you bleed crimson, Harvard is going to set you back $58,607 for tuition, room, board, and fees in the 2014–2015 academic year.

How did this happen? And who am I to argue with the forces of supply and demand? Well, in this case, we're not just talking about the supply of education. We're also dealing with the supply of *funding*. Much in the same way the federal government's belief that everyone should be a homeowner—and its policy reflecting this belief helped cause a housing bubble in the mid-2000s—its belief that everyone should have a college degree may have played a meaningful role in outsized education inflation.[4]

And how could it not? You don't have to get past Econ 101 to recognize that if the government makes it easy to pay tuition hikes through grants and subsidized loan programs, parents and students who believe education is a primary indicator of success will be happy—in some cases even desperate—to pony up.

At this point, however, it matters *less* how college got to be so expensive and *more* how to get a quality education that represents a good value.

Harvard versus Harford

I struggled with applying myself—academically anyway—in my last couple years of high school. As a result, my college options were limited. Community college offered me an excellent opportunity to begin my higher education while honing my scholastic skills.

After a couple years at Harford Community College, I was able to transfer all my credits to any school in the University of Maryland system, including my now alma mater, Towson University. While this route may not have been my first choice at the time, in retrospect it was an excellent way to get a quality education for an especially reasonable price. And by especially reasonable, would you believe that you can get an entire four-year undergraduate degree for the price of thirteen weeks at Harvard?

Indeed, the cost of tuition and fees at Harford Community College for sixty credits—two years of school—would be $7,488 at 2014–2015 academic year prices.[5] Assuming the student would complete his or her education at Towson University while living at home, the cost for two years of tuition and fees would be $17,180, again at 2014–2015 prices.[6] That brings the total cost of an undergraduate degree to $24,668, which wouldn't even cover the cost of a semester on campus at Harvard.

Is It Worth It?

This begs the question: In a day and age when the undergraduate degree has been commoditized and become viewed as a prerequisite for every white collar job available, do the intangible benefits from any collegiate scenario costing more than, say, $24,668 represent a good value proposition? Is the $200,000 premium or more (in today's dollars) that you pay for the elite private or Ivy League undergraduate experience worth it? Is the $100,000 premium you pay to live on campus at an out-of-state, public university worth it? Is the $50,000 premium you pay to live and eat on campus at your state university worth the cost?

The answer for any of the above may very well be an emphatic and justifiable *yes*. Please don't get the wrong impression. I'm not trying to suggest that Harvard isn't worth it, or that everyone should go the most economical route. Indeed, Harvard is entirely worth it for the student who will optimally benefit from the education itself, the life-shaping experience, the Ivy League credential, or perhaps the connections alone. Similarly, if you want to be a doctor specializing in internal medicine, it's likely worth it to pay Johns Hopkins University the $74,444 it costs for just your *first year of med school*.[7]

The value proposition for each student/school/benefactor combination will be different and worthy of exploration. Here's a four-step process that will help you make that determination and properly fund the resulting decisions.

The Nonconformist's Four-Step Education Savings Plan

Step #1: Determine if you are financially able

Can you afford it? This instruction is directed largely to parents, but the logic is identical and the process just as important for the many students flying solo in their educational endeavors. You may simply not have the income to maintain your household and save or pay for college at the same time. That's okay. You have more friends than you'd guess in the same boat.

If you're having trouble answering the question, "Can I?" without a more complete frame of reference, let me give you a rough idea of how much you'd have to save monthly, from the day your child is born for a full 18 years to have 100 percent of your financial needs met. This assumes the cost of education rises at 5 percent per year and you're able to earn 7 percent annually on your savings:

• Community college / In-state State U commuter:	$138 per month
• In-state State U commuter:	$192 per month
• In-state State U on campus:	$423 per month
• Out-of-state State U on campus:	$732 per month
• Premier private / Ivy League resident:	$1,310 per month

With that context, I must ask again: Can you afford it?

If you're a parent (or grandparent) struggling under the weight of this decision, please consider the following: It's actually irresponsible to prioritize your children's education over your present-day solvency and your future retirement saving. It would be much easier for a child to repay a student loan than to bail out parents with health issues who didn't save enough for retirement.

And how much school debt is too much? If you must incur debt to pay for school, try to keep the aggregate amount less than you can reasonably expect to earn in your first year's salary. Otherwise, it will almost surely be a strain financially.

Step #2: Determine whether or not you will choose to pay

Educational and financial institutions who run college savings plans may prefer you to believe that it's a cardinal sin to deny your children (or yourself) college funding, but that's because they have a vested interest. Deciding to help your children with education costs is an admirable choice, but it's still *your* choice. An unwillingness to offer your children a free ride doesn't make you a bad person.

Step #3: Develop a Family Education Policy

A Family Education Policy is the clear articulation of the answer to a question most parents will hear from their children at some point: "So, how much will you pay for my college education?"

As with many important questions in parenting, I recommend that you initiate a preemptive strike here. Don't wait until Johnny or Sally comes home to report what his or her friend's parents are going to pay for. Be the first to discuss this with your child.

You might, for example, offer to pay 100 percent of an in-state public university's costs if Junior keeps his grades up. But whatever you do, please don't write a blank check with the naïve response, "I'll pay for whatever school you can get into." The law of adverse selection suggests you'll end up paying top dollar for the warm-climate party school.

I recall one client, in particular, who had more than enough income to send each of his children to the school of their dreams. Instead, he used the context of college to send a parenting message. He and his wife offered to cover the financial costs of two years of education—the second two years. They wanted to ensure their kids were vested in their own educational decisions. They wanted to ensure their kids understood the value.

I'm not quite as tough. My wife and I have developed (and communicated) our own policy: we'll cover up to the cost of four years of in-state tuition at one of our excellent state universities. This doesn't mean we won't support our two boys financially if they choose to attend a private school or an out-of-state university. But we'll pay only for up to the price of an in-state state school.

They will bear any excess costs, and I'll encourage them to do so if they believe it will be in their long-term benefit.

And yes, if they're able to fall under Mom and Dad's financial aid cap, we will gladly donate the balance to the worthy cause of their choice, including a down payment on a home, a starter investment portfolio, grad school, or even travel.

Step #4: Develop a college savings plan

After you've determined that you're willing and able to pay for school, and you've articulated a Family Education Policy, it's time to start saving if you haven't already. Recalling our chart in Step #1, you'll need to save about $400 per month (every month, from the day your child is born, per child, earning 7 percent on your investments) in order to cover the expected costs of tuition, room, and board at an in-state public college or university. You can double that for most out-of-state public schools and triple it for elite private and Ivy League institutions. Simple, but not easy.

Where, then, should you save money for future education?

Navigating Route 529

529 college savings plans deserve your first look, and there are two types—prepaid plans and investment savings plans. Prepaid 529 plans offer you the opportunity to lock in the cost of today's tuition (only) in the state in which you live. The funds can typically be used for out-of-state schools, but the amount of aid will be based on the future cost of your state's schools. This option can make sense for families with older children because they don't have as long to save and wouldn't, therefore, have as high a probability of benefiting from an investment savings plan.

If you're getting started when your children are younger, consider a 529 investment savings plan, which offers a meaningful tax incentive and the opportunity to have the market pay off part of your kids' college expenses. From a tax perspective, these plans work like a Roth IRA. You contribute after-tax dollars to the plan, and then your contributions and any gains (hopefully) will be disbursed tax-free. In these plans, you invest in market instruments that come with a chance to outpace inflation, thereby reducing your net cost of college. Contributions are made after-tax, but gains are distributed tax-free for a fairly broad category of *qualified educational expenses*,[8] according to the IRS.

But there are a lot of different 529 investment savings plans. Which one should you use?

Investment savings plans are administered by state. Each has its own set of rules, expenses, investment options, and tax breaks, if applicable. You can use any state's plan, even if the student goes to a school out of state, but any applicable tax breaks may only be valid for your state's plan.

The plan that best replicates the investment philosophy espoused in the previous chapter is likely the Utah Educational Savings Plan, which features Vanguard and Dimensional's passively oriented, lower cost mutual funds. If your state's plan offers no tax benefits—or if the benefits appear minor in comparison to a plan with better investment options and/or lower expenses—don't feel tethered to your state.

Most importantly, I advise against using any plan that pays a broker a commission. Doing so cuts meaningfully into every dollar you invest. You can research all available 529 plans on helpful websites, for example, SavingForCollege.com. But be careful; they're not immune to conflict of interest either. Their "Find a 529 Pro" widget directs you to commission-based brokers who pay to be featured on the website.

Another helpful resource is Morningstar's annual roundup of, in their opinion, the market's best 529 plans.[9] You'll notice that all the top-tier plans are "direct," no-commission plans versus "advisor"-sold plans.

All that considered, 529 plans are still not a panacea. They don't deserve to be the sole receptacle for all of your college savings.

The 50 Percent Rule

Even if you have the wherewithal to save 100 percent of your college savings needs, consider not investing all of that money in 529 plans for the following reasons:

529 plans aren't perfect. Most don't include optimal investment options or ideal allocations for those investments. And, of course, the market isn't guaranteed to complement your education savings. You could actually lose money.

The states that administer 529s also aren't perfect. They could change plan rules or investment options—and, believe it or not, if you're using a prepaid plan, it's entirely possible that your state could struggle to fulfill their pledge to you.[10]

And I know you'll be shocked to hear this, but the federal government that presides over 529 plans—and their tax benefits, in particular—is also imperfect. In fact, in late 2014, President Obama put forth a proposal to tax 529 plan gains, which would have eliminated the primary reason for their existence. The outcry was loud and swift, and the planned tax hike was quickly but quietly dropped,[11] but the mere threat certainly weakens the entire 529 plan system.

In addition, Junior might get a scholarship and complicate the extraction of the funds without taxation. Of course, Junior could also decide that college is for the birds and hope to use the savings to buy a Harley and drive cross-country.

The good news, in that unlikely case, is that Junior wouldn't be able to withdraw the funds from the 529 plan—because it's your money, not his. You're the owner; he's merely the beneficiary. And you could actually change the beneficiary to his more scholastically inclined sister. The bad news is that if she decides to skip college as well, you'll be required to pay taxes and a 10 percent penalty on any gains in the plan in order to withdraw them. *Or*, you could always make yourself the beneficiary and go back to school.

How, then, can we account for all of this uncertainty? By invoking the "50 Percent Rule." Save only 50 percent of your estimated college savings needs in a 529 and leave the remainder in savings or your mid-term liquid investment account (chap. 7).

The truth is that if you have the funds to invest in your children's college education, after fully funding all of the financial priorities that stand before it (chap. 19), you're in the minority. Our next chapter addresses one of those financial priorities—retirement.

But if you're a parent, whether or not you can afford to fund your children's education, you can't afford *not* to address it.

Getting Creative

In determining the best course forward, for you or your student, it may well benefit you to get creative, to consider a course not prescribed by academia or your guidance counselor.

I'm a Tim Ferriss junkie. He's addicted to finding the most efficient ways to learn. Everything. He's the author of the best-selling 4-Hour series on work, health, cooking, and everything in between. He is an alternative education freak, which makes it all the more ironic that he received an undergraduate degree (in East Asian Studies) from Princeton.

If you're yearning for alternative education outside of the classroom, Ferriss is a great resource, as is Chris Guillebeau. "You don't have to live life the way others expect," says Guillebeau, the author of three books (all worthwhile reads), including his most recent, *The Happiness of Pursuit.*

Chris Guillebeau was a high school dropout who hacked his way into and through undergrad and graduate degrees only to discern that he could've learned a lot more for a lot less staying off the mainstream path. His experience inspired him to outline

"The One-Year, Alternative Graduate School Program," a complete educational experience all for under $10,000.

"The point isn't to disparage traditional education, but to provide an alternative for different kinds of learning," Chris says. "You never have to put off learning, and higher education isn't the only option."[12]

If higher education doesn't work for you for any reason, you have options. Trades, technical school, and—despite cultural messaging to the contrary—associates degrees are all viable alternatives that can lead to rewarding careers. Heck, even dropping out didn't work out so badly for Frank Lloyd Wright, Tom Hanks, Steve Jobs, and Bill Gates.

If you do choose the now conventional path of college, know that creativity can also help in the application process. While private schools have higher price tags, they also often have more generous endowments designed to attract unique and gifted students with meaningful discounts and scholarships.

Regardless, you'll get the most bang for your buck in any educational pursuit if you use the experience to enhance and magnify that which makes you uniquely you.

Simple Money Education Summary

1. Learning is priceless, but getting an education is a value proposition.

2. Yes, education can be very expensive, but it can also be surprisingly inexpensive. For the price of one semester at Harvard, you can get a degree from a prestigious state university as an in-state commuter who begins at a community college.

3. Parents, consider the following four-step plan to determine if and how to save for college:

    i. Determine if you are financially capable of helping your children with the cost of their college education.

    ii. Determine whether or not you will choose to offer "financial aid" for your children's higher ed.

    iii. Develop a Family Education Policy, the answer to the question, "So, how much will you pay for my college education?"

    iv. Develop a college savings plan—how much you'll need to save per month to meet your goals.

4. 529 education savings plans are valuable tools but don't deserve all of your college savings. Consider using them for only 50 percent of your savings.

5. If the traditional educational path doesn't work for you, you've got other options.

6. Use education to enhance what makes you uniquely you.

What INSIGHTS and ACTIONS did you take from this chapter?

11

RETIREMENT

The Wobbly Three-Legged Stool

WHY do I need to read this chapter?

The most reliable retirement analogy—the three-legged stool—is still helpful, even if a bit wobbly. It describes your path to retirement through three
primary sources of income after you stop working: a pension, Social Security,
and your personal retirement savings.

The (Wobbly) Three-Legged Retirement Stool

> You need to know the role that each of these income sources plays—or doesn't play—in your retirement planning. Are you working with a stable three-legged stool, or perhaps stilts, or a pogo stick?

Pensions

Corporate pensions—a stream of income pledged by the company for which you work—were once the strongest leg of the stool. Today, they are all but extinct. If you work for the federal government, a state, or a municipality, however, this leg of the stool may still exist.

If you have a pension, you likely have some options at your disposal. You may have the choice to accept your pension stream of income *or* receive a lump-sum distribution in its place. This is a challenging decision to make, and it must be based on several different factors. The largest factor is the financial solvency of the issuing entity. Most corporate pensions are underfunded, which means the company doesn't have sufficient money set aside to deliver on the promises it has already made to pension holders. This is reason for concern.

Most corporate plans do have an extra layer of protection through the Pension Benefit Guarantee Corporation (PBGC), a quasi-governmental pension insurance program of sorts. The only problem is that the PBGC doesn't always guarantee the entirety of the corporate pension pledges it underwrites. And the PBGC itself is also underfunded.

Most state pensions are also underfunded, but many are buoyed by their promisor's position as a taxing entity. Regarding fear of default, federal pensions are still the gold standard. They have an advantage. Unlike companies and states, they don't have to balance the budget—and they print the money. But in each pension scenario, it is important that you research and consider the implications of underfunding. This is especially true if you have a decision to make between a single lump-sum distribution and the stream-of-income option.

Please don't interpret my cautionary tone to suggest that you should necessarily take the lump sum over the income stream. A good pension is an incredibly valuable "asset," and an excellent stabilizing leg of the stool. Indeed, a pension that would provide $30,000 of income per year for the last twenty-five years of your life would be worth the equivalent of $422,818 today, sitting in an account earning 5 percent per year. If your pension also has an inflation adjustment feature, it is all the more valuable.

If you have a strong pension, or you don't have a lump-sum option with a questionable pension, you still have a number of choices to make. For example, pensions will typically offer benefit options, like "life only" and "life plus survivor," and many variations on those themes. The basic idea is that you could take a stream of income that would last as long as your life alone, or if you are married, you may elect the option that would continue to support your spouse for the remainder of his or her days. As you might guess, since the probability of one of two people in a marriage living longer is higher than the odds of only one, the life-plus-survivor option is typically going to pay out less money per period. But if you have a spouse, and they would need all or some of the pension income in the case of your passing, it's likely your best course of action would be to accept the smaller stream of income for both of your lifetimes.

Social Security

Each scenario needs to be reviewed individually, but having a third leg on your retirement stool, in the form of a pension, is a helpful and stabilizing force. Otherwise, your stool is just a pair of stilts. If so, your balancing act is hopefully grounded on one side with pledged income from Social Security.

Initially instituted in 1935 as a base level of income to keep retirees from falling into destitution, it could be argued that Social Security was never intended to be what it is today. And that's a primary source of income for many retirees throughout their retirement. After all, in its inaugural year, the average life expectancy of a male was just under 60, and Social Security didn't start paying until age 65.

This age of 65, denoted as Full Retirement Age (FRA), remained the norm for many years. Now, FRA is on a sliding scale. If you were born in 1937 or earlier, your FRA remains 65. But if you were born in 1960 or later, your FRA is 67. If you were born in between 1937 and 1960, your Full Retirement Age is somewhere between ages 65 and 67.[1]

Regardless of where your FRA lands, you may still begin receiving your Social Security benefit early—as soon as age 62—but at a discounted rate. The degree to which your benefit will be discounted is determined by your FRA. If you're in the 67 crowd and begin benefits at 62, you would receive only 70 percent of your expected FRA benefit, and your benefit would be discounted forevermore.

And there's another catch. The Social Security early retirement benefit is designed to work only for people who actually retire from a job that generates earned income. Any earned income you make over $15,720 (in 2015) begins to reduce your Social Security benefit, eventually eliminating it entirely. Therefore, it really only makes sense to take early Social Security if (1) you need the income, and (2) you don't have earned income over $15,720.

Once you reach Full Retirement Age, you can make as much money as you want and not suffer from any reduction in your Social Security benefit, but that doesn't mean it would be optimal to do so. This is because you can also delay the receipt of your benefit until as late as age 70. And why would you want to do that? If you can wait to take the benefit, the reward is a meaningful one for at least three reasons:

1. Every year you wait to take Social Security past age 62 offers an "investment rate of return" equivalent to earning 7 to 8 percent—guaranteed by the federal government. Would you accept a guaranteed rate of return on an investment at 7 percent? I would. This benefit continues to rise until you reach age 70, the latest point at which you can begin receiving your Social Security benefit.

2. Every year you continue to work further adds to your overall Social Security benefit, especially if you are finishing your career with a relatively higher income.

3. The benefits from the first two points are compounded by the fact that Social Security retirement benefits have a built-in cost of living adjustment. Yes, the government decides what it is, and no, it doesn't always reflect reality. It is, however, far better than a stream of income with no cost of living increase.

The bottom line? If you are retiring early and need the money— or you have good reason to believe your life expectancy is shorter than average—by all means, take it as needed. If, however, you're financially stable enough to wait to take Social Security, wait. Let it build. This "longevity insurance" will be a valuable tool in helping ensure that you don't run out of money in retirement.

And please don't leave any money on the table. There are many lesser-known Social Security provisions of which you might take advantage, most notably, the spousal benefit. This benefit allows lesser-earning spouses to receive whichever is greater—*their* retirement benefit or up to 50 percent of their partner's. That's right. Even a spouse who has *never* earned an income and never paid into the Social Security system is eligible to receive up to 50 percent of their *spouse's* benefit, even while their spouse receives 100 percent of their *own* benefit. The spousal benefit is only one of many provisions that might surprise you.

But take care; while the spousal benefit is only one of many provisions that might surprise you, we must also expect Social Security provisions to shift and change with the political winds. Two arcane strategies rising in popularity—"file and suspend" and "restricted application"—were recently killed by an act of Congress. Nonetheless, it is estimated that $10 billion in eligible Social Security benefits are left on the table every year. Don't let it be yours.

It is estimated that *$10 billion in eligible Social Security benefits*[2] are left on the table every year. Don't let it be yours.

Younger generations question whether or not they can count on Social Security at all. They believe that, like most pension plans, Social Security is underfunded. It is true that Social Security, after years of congressional raiding of the Social Security surplus, is now headed toward a deficit. However, I believe the "Social-Security-won't-be-here-for-me" fear is unwarranted. After all, the entity that doles out the benefits is the same entity that prints the money.

I acknowledge that this reality is not necessarily a comforting one, especially since the government magic show that creates money also has the unwelcome consequence of lessening the value of our dollars. But the United States is highly unlikely to default on its biggest financial obligation to its own citizens, if only for the reason that self-preservation wins every time in politics.

I do believe that younger generations can expect to see the value of their Social Security benefits reduced. In addition to the devaluation of the United States dollar, we should expect to see benefits means tested, resulting in potentially reduced benefits for higher-income retirees. It is also likely that we'll see the Full Retirement Age, already increased to 67, continue to rise higher.

The net effect is that younger generations are dealing less with a three-legged stool, or even stilts, in retirement. More and more they're left with a pogo stick. This makes them largely reliant on the third and final leg of the stool, Personal Savings, its own Pandora's box. Let's take a look inside.

Personal Savings

401(k), 403(b), 457, TSA, TSP, SEP, Simple, IRA, Roth. This is a not-quite-exhaustive list of different buckets into which retirement savers can shelter money for their future. It's written in code—IRS code, that is.

You see, retirement accounts—such as Individual Retirement Accounts (IRAs)—aren't investments, per se, but instead, investment receptacles, or buckets. Each bucket has a unique set of rules established by the Internal Revenue Service. These rules dictate how taxes are handled on money coming in and out. Various investments—stocks, bonds, mutual funds, cash, CDs—can be held inside the buckets, and the tax rules established for each bucket trumps whatever tax rules are associated with the individual investments.

Let's segregate the retirement buckets for now as Individual Retirement Accounts (IRAs) and employer-sponsored retirement plans:

IRAs—Traditional versus Roth

IRAs were created in 1974 to give American workers an opportunity—and an incentive—to save for retirement. In 2015, workers are able to save up to $5,500 per year, plus an additional "catch-up" allotment of $1,000 for savers 50 and older.

If you meet certain requirements,[3] contributions to a Traditional IRA are tax deductible. Growth inside the accounts is tax deferred. What is the price to be paid for this tax privilege? Well, it comes in a few forms—early illiquidity, forced taxes, and higher taxes on the back end.

Is it really a competition?

Feature	Traditional	Roth
Tax-Deductible Contribution	✓	
Tax-Free Withdrawals		✓
Penalty-Free Principal		✓
No Required Minimum Distribution		✓
Great Gift		✓

The illiquidity—or the lack of accessibility to your money—is an understandable feature. The government is giving you a tax break today to incentivize you to save for the future. So, if you touch the money before age 59.5 (with precious few exceptions), in addition to being taxed, you'll also pay a 10 percent early withdrawal penalty. The combination of federal, state, and local income taxes *and* the penalty can often halve your savings, making early distributions prohibitive. Compounding the prohibitive nature of early withdrawal penalties is that IRAs offer a level of creditor protection in most states, so if you're a visible member of the community or in trouble with creditors, your retirement accounts might be the only "safe" asset.

So, you *can't* take it out until after age 59.5, but you *must* take it out after age 70.5. It's called your Required Minimum Distribution, and whether or not you need the money, it's gotta come out. The penalty for not doing so is 50 percent of the required distribution! You didn't think the government would give you a tax deduction and indefinite tax deferral, did you? And don't think you can get out of it by dying before age 70.5 either. Your kids will have to pay the taxes, at what is likely a higher tax bracket than yours in retirement.

Additionally, when you take distributions, everything that comes out of the account is treated as ordinary income and will be taxed accordingly. This is disadvantageous if you own stocks and stock mutual funds—the primary growth vehicle for most retirement savers—because equities held for more than one year offer their own long-term capital gain tax privilege. Yes, the tax deduction on the front end is still worth it, but if you have the luxury of non-IRA investment savings, it may serve you well to overweight your equity holdings in taxable investment accounts that complement the equity tax privileges or a Roth IRA.

Speaking of the Roth, this little gem was brought to us by a senator of the same name who hails from a state known for its tax privilege, Delaware, in the Taxpayer Relief Act of 1997. From a tax perspective, the Roth IRA is the inverse of the Traditional IRA. There is no tax break on the front end, but distributions are tax free. Forever.

"I'm sorry, could you please say that in my good ear?"

Yes, it's true. And while your heirs would be forced to take Required Minimum Distributions (RMDs), they don't pay taxes on them either, making the Roth IRA the best gift you can give an heir. Meanwhile, neither you, the original saver, nor your spouse are required to make RMDs during your lifetime. Only use the money if you want or need it.

If it sounds like I'm biased in favor of the Roth IRA, it's because I am. There's an ongoing battle in the financial realm pitting the Roth IRA against its older cousin, the Traditional IRA. Most of the debate, however, is rendered irrelevant in my opinion because it doesn't consider the most important factor. The IRA debate as it stands is almost entirely about predicting taxes. As we've discussed, Traditional IRAs are taxed at the back end while Roth IRAs are taxed at the front end.

As the predominant logic goes, if you expect to be in a higher tax bracket in retirement than you are in today, contribute to a Roth IRA. If, instead, you are likely to be in a lower tax bracket in retirement, contribute to a Traditional IRA. By this math, if your tax bracket never changes, there's virtually no difference between the two investment options. But, like many personal finance one-liners and rules of thumb, this one falls woefully short of giving you the whole story.

Please consider this question: Which is more valuable—a dollar in a Roth IRA or a dollar in a Traditional IRA?

As long as you're expected to pay taxes, the answer to this question is *always* the dollar in the Roth. This is because the Roth allows you (and your heirs) tax-free growth *and* distributions free from taxes. The dollar in the Traditional IRA, on the other hand, is subject to taxation whenever you (or your heirs) remove it. So, if you're in a 25 percent tax bracket, your Traditional IRA dollar is actually worth only 75 cents. The higher your tax bracket, the less your Traditional dollar is worth.

In order for the Traditional-is-better logic to work, we must assume you'd take the extra cash on hand, which is an outgrowth of your tax deduction specifically associated with your Traditional IRA contribution, and invest it for your future retirement. If you make a $5,000 contribution to a Traditional IRA and you're in a 25 percent tax bracket, your deduction should be worth $1,250. In order for the Traditional to benefit you more than a Roth, you must not only be in a lower tax bracket in retirement, but you also must save that additional $1,250 for retirement at the time of your IRA contribution.

But what do most people do with their tax refund? Spend it!

What if you use your refund as a down payment on a car or for a vacation? The Traditional edge is eliminated. What if you didn't receive a refund at all? Unless you write a check to invest the amount you should have received as a deduction for your Traditional IRA contribution after Uncle Sam gives it back, the Roth wins.

One of the great frustrations in financial planning is that most of the planning is based on the assumption of things we can't actually control or change. These include annual income, inflation, market returns, and of course, taxes. So, you can contribute to a Traditional IRA, calculate the proportionate tax deduction, and invest that in a taxable account dedicated to retirement—every year—and hope the $17 trillion national debt somehow doesn't lead to tax increases. Or, you can take control of one of those factors and prepay your taxes using a Roth IRA, allowing you to ride off into the tax-free sunset.

Like so much of personal finance, the Roth/Traditional debate appears on the surface to be about numbers, but it's more about behavior. Again, personal finance is more personal than it is finance.

Employer Plans

As important as IRAs are for retirement savers, the majority of retirement saving today is done in employer-sponsored plans, the most visible of which is the 401(k). 403(b)s are the equivalent for nonprofits, and the Thrift Savings Plan (TSP) is the federal government's version of a 401(k).

The 401(k) plans have three primary components: an employee contribution, an employer match, and the potential for profit sharing, but the only one that is guaranteed is the first.

Employees may contribute up to $17,500 in 2015, plus an additional $5,500 for savers age 50 or older. Most 401(k) contributions are delineated as a percentage of your salary, and this is also how the employer match is handled. For example, you might save 10 percent of your salary, and the company matches 3 percent, for a total of 13 percent. Another common articulation of this match is "50 percent up to 6 percent." This, too, would be a 3 percent match, but it requires the employee to contribute more in order to receive the full match.

The match is "free money," a guaranteed rate of return on your investment simply for contributing. Do not leave free money on the table!

I repeat:

> DO
>
> NOT
>
> LEAVE
>
> FREE
>
> MONEY
>
> ON
>
> THE
>
> TABLE.

The final way to get money into your 401(k) comes in the form of profit sharing. This occurs when your company elects to share a portion of its profit with its employees. Please make sure to say thank you. This is behavior we'd like to encourage!

Until the mid-2000s, there were only traditional 401(k) plans. But now Roth 401(k) options are becoming more the norm. Here's how they work:

If your plan offers both a regular and Roth 401(k) option, you are making a choice between having your contributions made on a pre-tax basis—similar to a Traditional IRA and similarly taxed on the back end—or after-tax in a Roth contribution, right inside of your 401(k). Now you'd have two different buckets inside of your 401(k), but any employer match or profit sharing will go only into the traditional bucket.

How to decide whether or not to contribute to the Roth bucket, and if so, how much? First, if you are just getting started in your career and in a low tax bracket, going with the Roth is an easier decision to make than if you're in a higher tax bracket and counting on the traditional 401(k) contribution to reduce your taxable income. But, if you're in that higher tax bracket, it's also possible you make too much money to contribute to a regular Roth IRA because of the income caps.[4] In that case you may well want to take advantage of the Roth 401(k) opportunity. If you're stuck between the two, employ the wisdom of Solomon and split your contribution down the middle.

I'm thankful for the incentives the government has created to encourage us to save for retirement, and I hope you'll take full advantage of them. Remember, also, that these opportunities send an implicit message: "We—the government—want to help you take care of yourself because we can't or won't."

As the sun sets on pensions and Social Security's security is questioned, personal retirement saving is becoming an increasingly important leg of the stool. Having a wobbly retirement stool also begs the question, should we consider a fourth leg to stabilize it?

If you're self-employed or a small business owner . . .

you actually have some additional retirement saving options at your disposal. Your decisions will be driven by the amount you're able to save. If you're not able to save more than $5,500, it's likely best to put what you can into a Traditional or Roth IRA. If you can save about $12,500, the Simple IRA may be your best bet. Or, if you're able to save between $12,500 and up to $53,000, consider the SEP IRA or individual 401(k). Each of these has its own rules and tax ramifications and should be reviewed with your CPA and financial advisor before jumping in.

Annuities—a Fourth Leg?

"There are no bad investment products, just bad uses for them." This is marketing balderdash whipped up by someone promoting the sale of bad products. While there are certainly inappropriate uses for good products, there are also investment products that need never have been created. When combined with ignorance or self-deception, they can have disastrous results.

While every major branch of the financial services industry— banks, brokerage firms, and insurance companies—are or have been the proprietors of bad instruments, there's little question that "annuities," a product subheading under the insurance umbrella, have attracted the most criticism. They've even earned the anonymous tagline, "Annuities are not bought, they're sold," and while I admit that the tagline was likely written in an effort to market an annuity alternative, it rings a great deal truer than the "no bad products" quote.

Annuities are often promoted as a fourth leg of the retirement planning stool—or at least as an alternative leg—but do they hold up?

Types of Annuities

Since the word *annuity* has generic applications outside of the investment universe, for the purposes of this book, *an annuity is an investment product created by an insurance company.* There are four primary varieties of annuity common in the marketplace: immediate annuities, fixed annuities, variable annuities, and equity indexed (or just simply indexed) annuities.

An immediate annuity is a product in which you trade a lump sum of money for a stream of income from an insurance company. A fixed annuity has characteristics similar to those of a certificate of deposit (CD) with a bank, although the terms are typically longer. A variable annuity has characteristics similar to those of a mutual fund or mutual fund portfolio. An indexed annuity is, in reality, a fixed annuity advertising gains indexed to the upside of equity markets without the downside. If your too-good-to-be-true bells are going off, it's for good reason.

Annuity Pros

Please don't mistake my skepticism as blind condemnation of all annuity products. Annuities come with benefits that often cannot be duplicated in any other investment. Immediate annuities are, in my opinion, the most useful of the suite. For many people who will not be retiring with a meaningful stream of pension income, immediate annuities offer that potential. Because they are returning both interest and principal, the distributions are likely to be higher than anyone could justify taking from a balanced portfolio of investments. They can, in the right circumstances, be a valid replacement for the pension leg of the stool.

Another similar annuity product, the deferred income annuity, also may serve a valuable purpose—longevity insurance. For retirees concerned that they might outlive their money, deferred income annuities require a deposit today but don't begin paying until years in the future. If you're planning (with good reason) to be around to have your birthday celebrated on a Smucker's jar, it's possible that a deferred income annuity could offer some sleep-at-night peace. Fixed annuities allow an investor to lock in rates of return comparable to CDs, but likely for longer terms. If—when—interest rates rise from abnormally low rates to abnormally high rates, it could be a wise time to allocate some fixed income exposure to a fixed annuity. And unlike a CD, where interest is paid out and taxed annually, the interest or gains earned in annuities are deferred until distributions are taken.

Many annuities promise some level of principal protection. Even in certain variable products, a portion of your principal or even future income may be guaranteed by the issuing company. Not losing money is generally a good thing.

Regarding advantages of equity indexed annuities, uh . . . well, whoever sells you the policy will likely be going on a nice vacation soon. The commissions on these products range into double-digit percentages. Additionally, you could suspend disbelief and allow yourself to think you're getting the upside of the market without any downside. Ignorance can be blissful, if only momentarily.

Annuity Cons

Unfortunately for each of the pros, there are significant cons. At this time, prevailing interest rates (and correspondingly the rates used to calculate immediate annuity payouts) are so low that to commit funds could expose you to a meaningful amount of inflation risk. So even if you're predisposed to lock in a more secure income stream with an immediate annuity, consider waiting until rates normalize. The same could be said for most fixed annuities.

The tax deferral of annuities is worth something, but there's a price—or prices, really—to be paid. All of your gains will be taxed at your ordinary income tax rate. Especially if you're investing in a variable annuity with equity exposure, you're trading the tax privilege of capital gains for a rate—deferred or not—that could be twice as much.

Another negative tax implication is the loss of a "step-up" in cost basis to your heirs. Capital assets—like stocks and real estate, for example—that were purchased at a low cost are afforded a step-up in their cost basis upon your death. If you had sold those assets during life, you'd have paid capital gains tax. If you gave them to your heirs while you were alive, your heirs would inherit your cost basis. But if you wait to pass them to heirs until after your death, they will receive a step-up in their basis to the cost of the holding on your date of death, giving them an opportunity to sell those assets tax free.

Annuities with significant appreciation, however, receive no such benefit. In fact, not only will your heirs inherit your cost basis, they'll be paying tax at their ordinary income rate and may be forced to distribute the policy and take that gain in short order, resulting in a tax time bomb for those you hope to bless with an inheritance.

Simple Definitions

- **Cost basis**—The amount you paid for an asset, plus any investments you've made in improvements.

- **Capital gains (and losses)**—The difference between your selling price and your cost basis. If you sell for more than your cost basis, it's a gain; if less, it's a loss.

- **Step-up (in cost basis)**—Typically refers to a selection of the largest United States companies, best represented by the S&P 500 Index.

- **Capital asset**—"For the most part, everything you own and use for personal purposes, pleasure, or investment," surprisingly simply put by the IRS.

- **Asset class**—A collection of investments with similar characteristics; could be as broad as "stocks" and "bonds" or as specific as "Japanese small cap value."[5]

More Cons?

While the guarantees in some annuities are comforting, even if they're only made by the company (not the federal government), you may end up paying dearly for them. Many annuities offer a cafeteria plan of shiny options, but each comes with a cost. The insurance on your investments is not free.

My least favorite feature of annuities, however, is the illiquidity. First, you must be 59.5 years of age to withdraw the gains from an annuity and avoid paying tax on the gains as well as a 10 percent early withdrawal penalty. Second, because actuaries need time to make assumptions work and insurance companies need time to recoup the larger-than-average commissions to agents, most annuities tie your hands with a surrender charge. That can be a meaningful reduction in your payout, which usually descends over five, seven, or even up to fifteen years.

Finally, because you're paying for tax deferral by taking a tax hit upon distribution, many investors are understandably afraid to take the money out. This is true because annuities are taxed on a LIFO basis—last-in-first-out—which means that the gains (100 percent taxable) are distributed before the tax-free principal, unless you convert the product into an immediate annuity.

If you decide to purchase an annuity for any of their applicable uses, I recommend hunting for a low- or no-commission product with little to no surrender charge. This will help eliminate a couple of the most unfavorable qualities of these products. But even then, there still may be more cons than pros.

Unfortunately, the annuity sales process is notorious for capitalizing on fear and greed. This is a strategy used too often by every branch of the financial services industry, especially in the world of retirement planning. But any time you get a whiff of these decaying emotions—anytime someone is pressuring you to buy something with an urgent plea—that's a good indication that you should walk away.

Wisdom is never in a rush, and no financial product can buy you Enough.

Simple Money Retirement Plan Summary

1. Corporate pensions, once the strongest leg of the retirement three-legged stool, are all but extinct. The value of a financially solvent pension supported by a strong entity is high, but all of your options should be carefully considered.

2. Social Security, the second leg of the stool, was never intended to be our primary source of retirement income, but projections suggest it will become even less beneficial for workers many years from retirement. As long as you're healthy and able to continue working, waiting to take the Social Security retirement benefit will increase its advantages.

3. The third leg of the retirement planning stool is personal savings—Individual Retirement Accounts and company-sponsored retirement plans, like 401(k)s. The weakening of the first two legs of the stool put a lot of pressure on the third leg. Take advantage of "maxing out" your 401(k) and, in most cases, a Roth IRA.

4. Annuities are oversold, but that doesn't mean they should be ignored entirely. Immediate annuities—and especially deferred income annuities—may help stabilize a wobbly retirement stool.

What INSIGHTS and ACTIONS did you take from this chapter?

12

FINANCIAL INDEPENDENCE

The New Retirement

WHY do I need to read this chapter?

The topic of retirement strikes at the heart of Enough. And more than most, because it directly addresses the fear of not actually having, well, enough. In chapter 6, we took a look at where you stood according to Fidelity's retirement index. In this chapter, we're going to go further.

I'm going to give you more individualized guidance for how to view retirement (and saving for retirement) for future retirees who are currently in their 20s, 30s, 40s, and 50s, as well as those who are glimpsing retirement on the not-too-distant horizon. We'll conclude with a Retirement Stress Test for investors who want to get an initial indication if they are ready to retire. What's more, I'll offer two "silver bullets"—ways that you can give your personal retirement plan a boost if you're starting to think you'll never be ready. Think of it as your own personal bailout plan.

Commencement

What comes to mind when I say the word "RETIREMENT"?

The most common answer I get to that question is also the word's simplest definition: "Not working."

But is that really all retirement is? *Not* doing something? Do we really want to define the last thirty years of our lives—give or take—as being dedicated to the absence of activity?

Another couple of the most common responses I get are "freedom" and "doing whatever I want." But does that mean today—and for the majority of your adult lifetime—you're operating in bondage? Doing something that you don't want to do?

No.

In the words of the eminent philosopher, Ty Webb—Chevy Chase's character in the not–Oscar-nominated classic, *Caddyshack* —"This isn't Russia." You're not imprisoned today, and be sure that when you wake up, you are in complete control of your day, every day.

When we graduate from high school or college, the occasion isn't referred to as retirement (from learning), but as commencement. Something new. What if we viewed retirement not as the end of something, but the beginning? Or better yet, as the continuation of a life well lived?

Retirement . . . at Twentysomething

Commencement is not hard for twentysomethings to envision, but retirement is. Every semester I taught the "Fundamentals of Financial Planning" at Towson University, I asked for the students' gut reactions to the word "retirement," just as I did from you. Would you believe that most of the soon-to-be accountants and financiers had a generally negative impression of the concept?

The top two reasons: *

1. They have visions of hot, humid, early buffet dinners in rural Florida.
2. They consider the notion of traditional retirement to be out of their reach.

They hear that pensions are gone and Social Security is in trouble. They see their parents struggling to realize their own retirement goals. They think they're going to have to work forever.

Retirement seems just too far off for twentysomethings to reflect on seriously. How ironic, then, that their distance from retirement is also their advantage. Time is on their side.

Consider for a moment two future retirees—Jill is 20 years old, and her cousin, Jack, is 30. Always the early bird, Jill starts saving for retirement right out of the gate, investing a healthy $10,000 each year beginning at age 20 for 10 years. Then she stops investing. Jack decided to "live a little" and waits to begin saving until his 30th birthday, but he dedicates himself to saving $10,000 *every year* until his presumed retirement age, 70. Jill invests for only 10 years while Jack dedicates himself to investing for 40 years.

If each earns an annual average of 8 percent on their investments, which of them has more money to show for it at age 70?

- $3,147,136 (Jill)
- $2,590,565 (Jack)

How could that be possible? Jill invested only $100,000 to Jack's $400,000, but she ends up with $556,571 *more* than Jack at age 70. That is the story of compound interest. That is the benefit of getting a head start.

Of course, you might not be able to invest $10,000 per year beginning at age 20, but the point is to invest whatever you can as early as you can. Let the money work for you over time.

What about the grandfatherly wisdom of investing 10 percent of your income each year? Will you be okay if you just save 10 percent of your income for retirement every year? Probably, but there's a catch.

Let's say Jill began her career at age 22 with a starting salary of $50,000. She worked for 45 years, retiring at her Social Security Full Retirement Age of 67. She received a 3 percent raise annually and saved 10 percent every year, earning an annual average of 8 percent on her investment.

In this case, Jill would retire with $3,038,996 in retirement savings and a final year's salary of $183,573. According to the Fidelity retirement study (chap. 6), she'd need to have eight times her salary at age 67. She doubled that. Jill might reasonably expect to withdrawal 4 percent of her portfolio's balance in retirement, or $121,560, in year one.

There's only one problem with the 10 percent annual savings rule, but it's a big one: life doesn't always do what we want it to. It might be easy to save 10 percent when you can live happily off Ramen noodles and canned tuna at age 22. It may be even easier if you're a young married couple with two incomes at age 25. But what happens after you start piling up responsibilities? When your income decreases and your expenses rise after the miracle of birth generates a new dependent? When you have three kids and two of them are in college at the same time?

Life is variable, and so is your ability to save. For this reason, I recommend you aim to save 15 percent to 20 percent of your household income pre-kids, getting a great head start. Anticipate your savings rate may recede into the single digits in your peak expense years. Then, once you're an empty nester, you should be able to back-end load your retirement savings in your peak income years as you head toward retirement.

In short, you can dramatically increase your chances of financial success in retirement—and drastically reduce your savings workload in the middle stages of your career—by getting off to a great start in your twenties. Here again, we see the benefit of automating the *Nudge* default system (chap. 8). If you start your adult life saving 15 to 20 percent of your income, your chances of maintaining a high savings rate are that much higher as the Rider trains the Elephant (chap. 3).

. . . at Thirtysomething

At age 30, Fidelity suggests you should have one-half of your current salary saved, and a full year's worth of pay by age 35. If you saved like Jill, you're likely ahead of the game, but what about Jack? He has some catching up to do. How about you? Will the 10 percent rule still apply if you start later?

With an estimated salary of $63,000 at age 30, if you saved 10 percent each year until you were 40, you will have amassed $110,906. Not bad, but $53,500 short of Fidelity's goal. If you remain dedicated to saving 10 percent every year, the news gets better, however. By age 67, if all of our assumptions hold true, you'll have $1,940,555 saved—a little over 10 times your final salary of $177,273. You pass the Fidelity test, but you may be flirting with danger in your future reality. After all, a lot could change between now and then.

The big issue to contend with in your thirties is the initial financial shock of child-rearing. If one parent stays home to be with the kids, you'll obviously see your income decrease. But even if you maintain two sources of income, you'll still see a meaningful chunk of income ceded to a childcare provider. Anticipate this challenge in your retirement planning.

What if you're behind in your savings and struggling to put away enough going forward? First, I'd remind you of the third guarantee in financial planning (chap. 8), failure, and its counterpart, grace. If you're behind in your savings, the next step forward should be to forgive yourself and rebuild the Elephant's self-confidence. Save as much as you can now. Hopefully at least as much as your employer will match in your 401(k) or equivalent retirement plan. Then dedicate yourself to saving a significant portion (like 50 percent) of every raise or bonus you get until your savings rate approaches where it needs to be to fund a comfortable future.

A meaningful effort will help you feel the comfort of Enough even if you don't yet have enough.

. . . at Fortysomething

So you're old enough to have finally purchased *the* house and made it a home. You've molded your children into fine readers and artists, as well as gifted piano, soccer, and lacrosse players. You're on the board of the local YMCA, you support the PTA, and you normally make a contribution to the offering plate when it's passed at church.

How about your retirement plan—how is that progressing? Do you have an inherent tendency that makes saving easy, or is it more difficult? You'll recall from chapter 7 that each of us has a saving personality on a continuum spanning a wide spectrum.

How does your cash flow personality impact retirement?

By the time you're into your forties, it's likely that your retirement savings is reflective of your cash flow personality.

Most educators in the realm of personal finance take aim solely at those on the left side of this continuum as if more is always better. But is it possible that you could actually save too much for retirement? Absolutely. I'm not demonizing any particular level of net worth, but you may be socking away as much as humanly possible for your future to the detriment of your (and your family's) present. Many advisors, driven by their economic bias to manage your money, will use the save-for-your-family's-future guilt trip to wrench more of your dollars into accounts they can oversee.

Of course, most of us are actually more inclined to lean in the direction of the spendthrift than the hoarder. It's easy to overvalue the present because we can see, touch, and feel it today. And fortysomethings have so many pressing concerns demanding attention and funding, it's only natural for deferred gratification to take a backseat. So my call for balance between your future and present plans should not be received as permission to underestimate the importance of saving for the future. The reality is that you should have three times your current salary saved by the time you reach age forty-five. And four times your salary when you reach your fiftieth birthday, according to Fidelity. That requires a concerted effort.

One of the best examples I've seen of properly balancing money and life comes from a good friend of mine (and financial planning colleague). He is living with and battling Cystic Fibrosis, a disease that attacks the lungs and leaves those so afflicted with a life expectancy of 37.4 years. My buddy is married with two beautiful children and turns forty this year. He's forced to be focused on the future for his family's sake (and hopefully for his sake as advances in medicine push toward a cure for CF), but he also recognizes the absolute necessity of getting the most out of every single day.

Tomorrow is surely coming, but it's promised for none of us, and our retirement planning should reflect that dichotomy.

. . . at Fiftysomething

The fifties are a transition decade for most retirement savers. At the front end, you're holding on for dear life, attempting to survive life's most expensive stretch—the kids' college years. But then, one day dawns empty nest–hood. Hopefully.

This is an important stage at which to take stock of your retirement readiness. Where do you stand? Are you behind schedule? If so, don't panic—let's see how bad it really is.

At 50, our friend, Jack, has $388,487 in retirement savings—3.5 times his $110,500 salary. Fidelity wants him to be at four times his salary. He's close enough to this goal that if he continues to save 10 percent of his income, and the market treats him reasonably well, he'll enter his next decade on track for retirement.

However, what if Jack had the same level of savings, but he was three years older and making more money—say, $150,000. Then, at age 55, he'd have only 2.5 times his current salary, half of what Fidelity recommends at that age. But watch this: If he bumps his savings rate up to 20 percent—a savings rate he can afford now that the kids are (mostly) independent—he'll catch up to Fidelity's retirement savings recommendations by the time he reaches 67.

The moral of the story? There's still time to catch up in your fifties if you dedicate yourself to saving in your peak income years.

Retirement Stress Test

Once you've moved into your sixties, you're officially in the retirement home stretch. But please don't misread me. I don't want you to stop working. I just want you to be *able* to stop working in case you want to—or need to for health reasons.

At this point, I want you to work because you want to, not because you have to. That's the definition of financial independence.

Let's see how close you are to this milestone with a simple Retirement Stress Test. You'll recall from the previous chapter that the three-legged stool of retirement is composed of three different potential income sources:

- Pensions
- Social Security
- Personal Savings

In order to complete the stress test, all you'll need is a recent statement for each. Adding your expected income from any pensions and Social Security will indicate your amount of fixed income. Since these numbers are typically formatted as monthly income, multiply each by 12 to arrive at an annual expected income from fixed sources. If, for example, you're expecting $1,200 per month from pensions and $2,300 of combined household Social Security income, you'd have $42,000 of fixed income. Not a bad start.

$$(\$2,300 + \$1,200) \times 12 = \$42,000$$

Now, let's take a look at your personal savings. In order to determine a rough estimate of how much income you could reasonably expect to take from your retirement savings buckets—like 401(k) plans and IRAs—multiply the sum of your aggregate retirement savings by 4 percent, or .04. For example, if you have $400,000 in a 401(k), $525,000 in a Traditional IRA, and $75,000 in a Roth IRA, we could reasonably expect your savings of $1,000,000 to generate $40,000 of annual income.

$$(\$400,000 + \$525,000 + \$75,000) \times .04 = \$40,000$$

If we add the fixed income sources to the reasonable annual withdrawal amount from your personal savings, we can estimate annual income of $82,000. If $82,000 is greater than your annual income needs, that's a good sign.

Mind you, your assets are not guaranteed to outlive you just because you passed the retirement stress test. A more detailed analysis, which takes into account taxes and market volatility, is a must. But at least you've passed the first test.

What if you failed the test? What if you know your income needs are higher than the stress test estimates you'll be able to support? Simply put, there are really only two options: You need to spend less money or make more. If you are behind, here are two retirement planning "silver bullets" that could help you get on track.

Silver Bullet #1

The first retirement silver bullet may be the most powerful: *move to a lower cost of living area.*

This maneuver is especially impactful when contrasting areas with the highest cost of living to those with the lowest. According to www.bestplaces.net, an online resource estimating the cost of living in areas across the country, the median home price in Chevy Chase Village, an idyllic Washington, DC, suburb in Maryland, is $1,493,400. Additionally, the cost of living is 252 percent higher than the United States average. Alternatively, the median home price in economically battered Detroit is $35,700. There, the cost of living is 26.70 percent lower than the United States average.

But if that comparison appears all too convenient and unrealistic, consider this contrast: Baltimore suburb Parkton, Maryland, boasts a median home price of $439,300 and a cost of living 52.10 percent higher than the United States average. Meanwhile, Knoxville, Tennessee, the lovely home of the University of Tennessee, has a median home price of $109,200 and a cost of living 19.30 percent lower than the national average. And it's on the water and doesn't snow as much.

Since I'm sure Jill isn't behind on her retirement saving, let's picture Jack and his wife living in Parkton, trying to figure out their plan for retirement:

In Parkton

- Their home is now worth $500,000.
- They have a $200,000 mortgage (from college costs and home improvements).
- They need $100,000 of income to cover annual expenses:
   - Their mortgage principal and interest payment (a $200,000 loan at 5 percent for 15 years) is $19,000 per year.
   - Without a mortgage, their income need is only $81,000.

- Jack took a pension lump-sum offer. They now have total retirement assets of $800,000. At 4 percent, they could reasonably expect to take $32,000 of income from personal savings.

- **With an additional $18,000 from Social Security, they can reasonably expect a total of $50,000 in retirement income, only 50 percent of their estimated need.**

In Knoxville

- They were able to purchase a comparable home for $200,000, mortgage free.

- The additional $100,000 in net proceeds from the home sale brings their retirement nest egg to $900,000, capable of producing annual income of $36,000.

- According to cost of living ratio, it would require only $45,360 in income in Knoxville to feel like the $81,000 they want to live comfortably in Parkton.

- **With an additional $18,000 of income from Social Security, their $54,000 in annual income now represents 119 percent of their estimated need.**

If you find yourself in a retirement planning pickle, I'm not suggesting you read this and hammer a for-sale sign into your yard. *Cost* of living should not be confused with *quality* of life, and if your geography and proximity to friends and family is where you derive the most joy, it's not my suggestion that you have a financial duty to uproot. But, if you've reached a retirement planning dead end and find yourself without options, and a yearning for a refreshing change of pace, there is no question that transplanting your financial life to a lower cost of living area can transform a bleak retirement plan into a surprisingly comfortable one.

Silver Bullet #2

You do still have another option, and much as Silver Bullet #1 was summed up in one word—*move*—so too is Silver Bullet #2—*work*.

It's not what you think. If you're one of the many who've dutifully labored for a lifetime, largely motivated by some point in the future when you'd be able to dance your way out of your office never to return, I'm not intending to obliterate that daydream. In fact, the only way this second silver bullet will work is if you're able to find—or create—a vocation that gives you as much or more joy than being fully retired.

And this isn't just advice coming from your financial planner but also your doctor, as Anne Tergesen illuminated in her 2005 *Businessweek* cover story entitled, "Live Long and Prosper. Seriously."[1] She quotes Dr. Jochanan Stessman, head of the geriatric and rehabilitation department of Hadassah-Hebrew University Medical Center, as saying, "There's a strong argument for continuing to work throughout life."

This doesn't mean you have to work full-time, nor does it mean that you should be doing work that drains you. This is your license to create your dream job and begin to plan a phase of life we'll call pseudo-retirement. You're working enough to keep your mind and body functioning at high levels, with enough income to reduce your need to tap your nest egg.

Let's look at this in the context of our hypothetical retiree from Silver Bullet #1:

With two incomes, Jack and his wife are currently making $175,000 in income, $75,000 more than they need. But they're burned out and want to retire—yesterday. Unfortunately, if they take their early Social Security benefit at their current ages and rely on their nest egg to fund the remainder of their $100,000 income need, they'll be pulling 10.3 percent out of their personal savings. That's an unsustainable withdrawal amount and could sink their

How can Jack and Jill retire?

Age of Couple:	62	
Assets		
	- Home:	$500,000
	- Nest Egg:	$800,000
Liabilities		
	- Mortgage:	$200,000
Income Need:		**$100,000**
Retirement Income		
	- Social Security:	$18,000
	- Nest Egg @ 4%:	$32,000
	- **Total Income:**	**$50,000**

retirement ship before it even sets sail. Here's the recommended course of action:

1. At age 62 . . .

- They begin to plan their dream job, while contributing $50,000 of their $75,000 in excess income to their nest egg.
- They aggressively pay down their mortgage with $15,000 per year of excess annual income. Dial back the aggression in the portfolio and lower the rate of return expectation to 5 percent.

2. At age 66 . . .

- They transition to their dream jobs, accepting lower pay—$100,000—for full-time jobs they more fully enjoy.
- They stop saving for retirement but delay taking Social Security, allowing future income to grow.
- Their mortgage has been paid down to $94,093. Cease extra principal payments.
- They allow their nest egg—now $1,187,911—to grow, conservatively invested to earn 5 percent per year.

187

3. At age 70 . . .

- They scale back to part-time work at their dream jobs.
- Their mortgage balance is now $31,062.
- They take their Social Security benefit, now at $30,927. With part-time income of $50,000, total current income is $80,927.
- The nest egg is now up to $1,436,620.

4. At age 72 . . .

- The mortgage is now paid off, reducing their income need by $19,000 per year.
- Their Social Security benefit is now $32,176 (assuming 2 percent inflation per year).
- Their nest egg is now $1,583,873. Four percent income is now $63,354.
- Their income need with inflation considered is now $98,738.
- **Their Social Security plus 4 percent portfolio income is $95,530, giving them enough income to live comfortably.**

Please remember that working part-time in retirement does not represent failure. It represents a new reality. As a culture, we're retiring earlier and living longer than our predecessors. This puts more pressure on our income generation and necessitates an evolved retirement strategy.

Also consider that the purpose of retirement is not necessarily to *not* work but to do the work of your choosing. As Confucius said, "Choose a job you love, and you will never have to work a day in your life." Maybe you've never had the chance to put that wisdom to the test. Ironically, there's no better time than in retirement.

Reducing Retirement Stress

What's the rush, anyway? In addition to research that finds work good for your health, the Harvard School of Public Health concluded that rushing into retirement is bad for it. In the ongoing US Health and Retirement study, they discovered that "those who had retired were 40 percent more likely to have had a heart attack or stroke than those who were still working."[2]

Why is this planned utopia one of the most stressful events in life, consistently ranking up there with public speaking—and fear of death?[3]

Change. Fear of the unknown. A diminished sense of purpose. A decrease in human interaction.

For this reason, I recommend that anyone planning to retire—regardless of their financial wherewithal—do so with deliberate consideration and planning.

Consider the following process.

Simple Money Journal Entry

Preparing for Retirement

1. ***Think about it.*** Considering the magnitude of the retirement decision, isn't it interesting that it's usually the Elephant driving this decision—not the Rider (chap. 3)? This phase of retirement planning is intended to get the Elephant and Rider working together on this big project. To get the juices flowing, Carol Anderson of Money Quotient, the nonprofit research group specializing in the many behavioral elements in personal finance, suggests considering which of these statements apply to you:

   • I'm counting the days until I can retire.

   • I expect my retirement to be very different from what my parents experienced.

   • I don't want to retire "cold turkey."

   • I worry about not having enough money when I retire.

   • I wonder what I am going to do with my time when I retire.

- I worry that Social Security will not be available when I retire.
- I haven't thought much about what I want to do when I retire.
- I like being productive and would like to continue working after I retire.
- I'm worried that my health will fail when I retire.
- I have a clear vision of how I will invest my time and energy when I retire.

2. **Plan for it.** Now let's start moving into the realm of the practical. What would life actually look like in retirement? Not the first week, but the thirty-first. What's the typical week in retirement for you? Write out your ideal week as well. Sunday through Saturday, what would you be doing morning, afternoon, and night?

3. **Practice it.** Now, put your planning to the test. Take a week of vacation (or two if you can manage it) and live out your typical, ideal week in retirement. Kick the tires.

One of the best ways to reduce the stress of retirement is to phase into retirement in stages. Even if you can "afford" not to, work part-time at first and use the balance of your time to pursue the activities that will eventually consume all of your time. If you do retire "cold turkey," remember that life is not a two-act play—backbreaking work followed by a passive retirement. Your adult life is (at least) a three-act play, and you're just beginning the second act. It's not until Act Three when life may take on characteristics more like a "traditional" retirement picture.

Recognize that retirement is a major life transition. As with any of these major milestones—marriage, parenthood, the loss of a loved one—the best insurance from crumpling under the weight of change is to enter it as a whole, healthy, and fulfilled being.

The optimal way to reduce the stress of retirement, therefore, is to enter it with Enough.

Simple Money New Retirement Summary

1. If you view retirement as a magic pill that will deliver all of your hopes and dreams, it's likely to disappoint.

2. With the disappearance of corporate pensions and the fear of losing Social Security retirement benefits, twenty-somethings feel as though they're on their own when it comes to retirement—and they might be right. But time is on their side.

3. If you start early, a linear 10 percent savings plan is likely to result in retirement success—but remember, life isn't linear. Kick-start your financial future with a higher savings rate out of the gate. It will help make up for what will likely be decreased savings in midlife.

4. Each decade of adulthood comes with its own unique retirement planning challenges—be ready to address them.

5. If you failed the Retirement Stress Test, there are really only two ways to improve your situation: decrease your expenses or increase your income.

6. Despite its utopian promises, retirement is one of the most stressful transitions you're likely to endure in life. Reduce this stress by retiring in stages and through thoughtful, deliberate planning.

What INSIGHTS and ACTIONS did you take from this chapter?

13

ESTATE AND LEGACY

Cheating Death

WHY do I need to read this chapter?

Without an ounce of exaggeration, I can confidently write that estate planning is *the most important element of all financial planning*. Yet, reportedly 80 percent of Americans don't even have the most basic estate planning documents.

"I'm too young to worry about that" or "I don't have enough money to be concerned about an 'estate'" are the types of reasons I hear from people who haven't checked off this whopper of a to-do. But I think it goes deeper than that.

In this chapter, I'll be addressing the real reasons people avoid estate planning and how to overcome these potent de-motivators. We'll discuss the three estate planning documents that every adult should understand and have drafted.

But first, here's why estate planning is so vitally important: Although the probability of a premature death is extremely low, *the damage it can do to one's plans for life and money without an estate plan can be catastrophic.*

For example, if you have minor children, it is your will that stipulates who should parent your kids if both spouses go down with the ship. If you don't decide, your state of residence will be happy to do that for you. The stakes are high.

The most important provisions in your estate planning documents have nothing to do with your money, or even your estate. When you get past the legalese—an unfortunate necessity—these are simply the most important love letters you'll ever write, an articulation of what you hope to be your legacy.

The Real Reasons People Avoid Estate Planning

Here are the real reasons people avoid estate planning:

1. They'd rather avoid the topic. They fear that discussing death might somehow hasten it. However irrational, this is a common and powerful de-motivator.

2. They see the probability of actually employing their estate plans "anytime soon" as exceedingly low. Although quite rational, this can be a fatal flaw (pun intended).

Responsibility for the first reason to avoid estate planning falls entirely on the shoulders of the Elephant (chap. 3). It's driven primarily by emotion and caring little for rationale. The rational Rider, however, is the one *over*thinking things in reason number two.

We can appeal to the Elephant by getting past the instinctive self-preservative response—the fear of death—and instead considering the compounded emotional destruction of inaction. Kids being shuttled in and out of court, potentially getting matched up with the wrong guardian. Default appointees doing their best to intuit a decedent's wishes but who are unqualified to do so. Even the most stubborn pachyderm can be motivated when asked to consider the worst-case scenarios of not completing an estate plan.

The Rider, focused on the overwhelming number of life's other obligations, has understandably underestimated the importance of estate planning because so many other tasks outrank it in apparent urgency. But as Stephen Covey has taught us, we must see through the seemingly urgent trees to behold the vitally important field beyond. It doesn't take much convincing to see that estate planning is so important that it *becomes* urgent. The Rider is quickly wooed into the estate planning process by the prospect of preserving an element of control in life even after death. Riders love asking and answering "What if?" questions, and that is the essence of estate planning.

After properly motivating the Rider and Elephant, they become a productive pair as we jump into the tangible output of estate planning.

Three Documents

There are three primary documents that make up a suite of necessities: a will, durable power of attorney, and an advance directive.

Will

Your last will and testament is the most important estate document and also requires the most effort. Done properly, it entails some avenues of thought you'd prefer to avoid, but its import can be seen immediately. This is especially true in determining the three offices commonly appointed in the document:

PERSONAL REPRESENTATIVE

The office that will apply in every circumstance is the Personal Representative (PR), still known as the Executor or Executrix in some states. The PR's job is to walk your estate through the probate process, which of course begs the question, "What is probate?"

When you're living, *you* own your assets. The moment you kick the proverbial bucket, your *estate* is the new owner of said assets. Probate is the state-specific process of transferring the assets in your estate to wherever your will stipulates they should go—your heirs, any trusts, or other entities. It's the PR's job to ensure that process happens.

Because of the legal complexity, many personal representatives will hire an estate attorney to aid them in the completion of their duties. Some future decedents, therefore, name an attorney for this office in the first place. If you choose a friend or family member, consider someone who is proactive and detail-oriented, if not verifiably anal retentive.

Guardian

The most important office for parents of minor children to fill is the Guardian, the legal equivalent of the religious office of godparent. The guardian effectively becomes the child's parent if both biological parents are deceased.

This is a huge responsibility that shouldn't be taken lightly by the person bestowing, or receiving, the nomination. It's especially important that you avoid letting this decision devolve into a popularity contest. Many people think their parents are a natural choice. Natural though it appears, it may not be wise. Your parents like being grandparents, and while they'd be honored (and would almost surely accept this responsibility), it likely isn't in your kids'—or your parents'—best interest. (See the "Don't leave us with the babies!" commercial.[1])

This decision is too important to worry about what other candidates for the job may think about *not* being asked. And while it is an imperative to seek permission of your designee(s), please remember that you don't actually have to tell people they *weren't* chosen. It'll likely never come up.

Instead, consider these questions: Who shares your values and has similar goals? This is a great starting point, but also consider practicality. Who is in close enough proximity that the kids wouldn't have to be uprooted? Who isn't already overwhelmed with several young children of their own? And most importantly, who would do a great stinking job?

TRUSTEE

The final office created in a will that we'll explore is that of Trustee. The trustee has the duty of watching over funds set aside for your minor children in trust. A trust is a non-person entity—a piece of paper given legal standing. You are able to specify an array of rules stipulating how the trust is to be managed, and it's the trustee's job to ensure that the beneficiaries of your trust(s) abide by those rules.

If I've lost you here because I mentioned the word *trust*—evoking notions of "trust funds" for which you're sure you don't qualify financially—please read on. This tool is valuable for and available to most families.

While there certainly are cases where a trust may exist during your life—for example, a Revocable Living Trust (RLT) or an Irrevocable Life Insurance Trust (ILIT)—the trust that has the broadest appeal in estate planning is the Testamentary Trust. A testamentary trust isn't created until you cease to exist. Only then is it funded, by the assets in your estate or via beneficiary designations.

While a guardian has only legal responsibility over a child without special needs until he or she reaches the age of majority, a trustee's responsibility extends as long as the trust exists, which is sometimes into perpetuity. But allow me to give you an example of a well-known family to help make more sense of this.

Ward and June have a testamentary trust created in their wills designed to receive all assets that are not in retirement accounts—most notably, the proceeds of their life insurance—for the benefit of their children, Wally and Theodore. If, heaven forbid, Wally and Theo lose both of their parents, Aunt Martha will assume the role of guardian and Uncle Billy will become the trustee of the newly created trust.

As most are, Wally and Theo's testamentary trust was written with broad powers to provide funding for their health, education, maintenance, and support at the trustee's discretion. Then, after the boys are fully independent, when Theo reaches age 25,

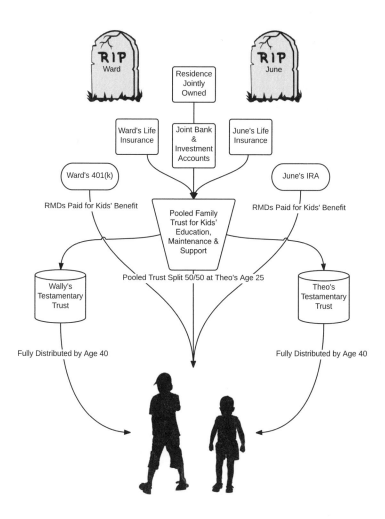

the pooled trust is split into two. One-half for each of the boys. Finally, the trusts will be fully distributed. One-third at age 30, half at age 35, and the remainder at age 40.

This is just one example, but in any case, the point is to protect the funds both *for* and *from* the children. It doesn't take much of an imagination to guess what many eighteen- or twenty-one-year-olds would do with a huge payday. So, by spreading out distributions, the impact of the money is lessened. Some parents choose to keep the money in trust indefinitely, preserving its contents against the unseen, like a failed marriage. The more money, the more care that goes into crafting the trust language.

I'm a big fan of Warren Buffett's strategy: Leave the kids "enough money so that they would feel they could do anything, but not so much that they could do nothing."[2]

You likely noticed that the ideal traits for a personal representative (detail oriented) may be different from those for a guardian (character shaping). The same is true for the trustee. This designee should obviously be good with money, but also wise enough to separate legitimate expenses from the foolhardy, and confident enough to express his or her wisdom in the face of a challenge from a persistent youngster (or adult).

While there may well be cases in which one person best fits all of these roles, in many scenarios, there will be different people in each position. Indeed, some recommend it as a matter of necessity to avoid conflicts of interest.

Further complicating matters, there should likely be second and even third designees for each office in case any of your primary appointees are unwilling or unable to serve.

These are challenging decisions for many reasons, but ultimately, drafting a will can be a heartening exercise as we remember times past and envision the future. Consider easing the inherent tension by scheduling a relaxing date night to follow your meeting with the attorney.

DPOA

But it's not time for dinner just yet. There are two other documents that should accompany your will, including a Durable Power of Attorney (DPOA). This document is designed to give someone else the ability to act on your behalf in financial matters if you are unable or unavailable to do so.

You're traveling for work while in the middle of a house purchase? Your agent can act on your behalf with a properly drafted DPOA. What makes this particular power "durable" is that it can be used even—if not especially—in the case that you are incapacitated, allowing your attorney-in-fact to move needed funds between bank accounts, for example, in the case of a disabling injury.

One of the past difficulties with power of attorney is that institutions fearful of being sued—banks, in particular—would not accept all documents upon presentation. There are a couple ways to ensure that the people you select will actually be empowered: First, you can register your documents with the institutions you deal with most often—your bank and investment manager, for example. The approval process may take a few weeks, but then your attorney-in-fact will have the ability to act on your behalf without hindrance. Second, the problem of delayed approval has become widespread enough that many states have created statutory power of attorney language. Therefore, ensure that your documents conform to the statutory language giving them the strength you intend.

Please note that a DPOA properly drafted and utilized is a very powerful document, and only to be put in trusted hands.

Advance Directives

So you can see how anyone with children or property would want a will, and how anyone with financial responsibilities would want a durable power of attorney. But this third document completes the trio of essential estate planning documents imperative for *anyone* over the age of majority—the Advance Directive.

This is a dual-purpose document with singular intent—to designate a person to make healthcare decisions on your behalf in the event you are unable to do so. Do you remember the story about my accident from chapter 4? When I was lying in the hospital unconscious, important medical decisions were being made that ended up impacting my very survival—but I wasn't able to make them.

"Once your child reaches the age of majority, your personal rights are terminated and you may not be able to make healthcare . . . decisions on your child's behalf," says Maryland estate planning attorney Jane Frankel Sims. Sims counsels that every parent should get their kids to sign an advance directive—along with a financial power of attorney—before they head off to college. But they're equally, if not increasingly, important for you.

An advance directive comprises two documents—a healthcare power of attorney and a living will. The healthcare power of attorney designates an agent to make healthcare decisions when you're unable. The living will, then, instructs your designee on how you would like end-of-life decisions to be made.

Sadly, you may have heard of the Terri Schiavo case. After suffering brain damage resulting from a massive heart attack in 1990, Schiavo was medically deemed to be in a "persistent vegetative state" from which there would be no recovery. Her husband said Terri's expressed desire was not to be kept on life support in such a situation, but he was opposed by her parents, who insisted she be kept alive. As a result, this most private of decisions was made increasingly public until a judge ordered the removal of Schiavo's feeding tube—in 2005.

Even in resurfacing that story for this explanation, it's heart-wrenching. I can put myself in the husband and the father's shoes and sympathize with both of them. But the advance directive helps ensure that there will be no sides taken, that you will be the sole arbiter of this decision.

If you are meeting with an attorney to draft your will, consider having them also draft your durable power of attorney and advance directive. But if your recent high school grad is headed out the door to college, you should be able to print an advance directive from your state's attorney general's website, or find it at www.caringinfo.org.

The Most Important Love Letters You'll Ever Write

When you think of the investment of time and money required to draft these documents optimally, it starts to add up. But when you consider them as they are—the most important love letters you'll ever write—you realize that the investment is well worth it.

Writing your final wishes on a napkin might work in the movies, but it's not a real-life option to be considered. Yes, you can pay $29.99 for will-making software or $69 for an online will service, but I invite you to consider that the output may be worth precisely what you put in.

Many employers offer prepaid legal services as a company benefit. This option introduces a vital element in the creation of estate documents—the human element. But be careful, because most of these programs are designed to provide cookie-cutter services. If you choose this path, use what you've learned in this chapter to ensure that your documents are customized to you.

The preferable option for preparing estate documents, however, is retaining the services of an attorney who specializes in estate planning. The cost and quality of such services ranges widely, so consider interviewing a few attorneys who come highly recommended by people you trust. Most attorneys bill on an hourly basis, but a flat-fee service, including the preparation of a will, durable power of attorney, and advance directives, will help ensure that you won't be afraid to ask questions. And be sure to demand answers in terms that you understand—not the language of legalese.

The Most Powerful Estate "Document"

After all the expenditure of time, effort, and money to get those essential estate planning documents drafted, signed, and notarized, you can sleep through the night—right? Well, not quite.

All that work could be for naught, unless you address a simple form: the beneficiary designation. It is associated with any retirement accounts, annuities, or life insurance policies. Believe it or not, these forms will trump the wishes in your will if they differ.

I learned of one such precedent, and it's brimming with karmic irony. Bill, we'll call him, left his wife of many years for his secretary. After reluctantly ceding the requisite 50 percent of his assets in the divorce, he immediately updated his estate planning documents to ensure that his new squeeze would get the remainder. Then, in the middle of his backswing at Pebble Beach, he was struck dead.

Unfortunately—depending on your perspective, I suppose—Bill had forgotten to change the beneficiary designations on his retirement accounts and life insurance. That's right—100 percent of the proceeds from these went to his now ex-wife.

A more wholesome example, and one that I see regularly, involves young married couples who still have Mom and Dad listed as their beneficiaries. The moral of these stories is to check your beneficiaries at least annually. This is especially important in the financial services realm, where mergers and acquisitions are changing the sign on the door regularly. It's important to make sure this powerful estate planning form is accurate and up-to-date.

Estate versus Legacy

Our estate is not to be confused with our legacy. *Estate* is a legal term defined as "the degree, quantity, nature, and extent of interest that a person has in real and personal property."[3] In other words, it's your accumulated stuff. Our *legacy*, however, is the intangible, collective impact we have on the world around us.

On the way to the church for a funeral, I wasn't optimistic. I was hunting for a silver lining and couldn't find one. Melanie's husband—Natalie and Gabe's father—was only thirty-six when he died.

Nick Selvi was thirty-four years old when he was diagnosed with stage 4 rectal cancer. A longtime musician, he was teaching elementary school music and leading the fifth-grade jazz band, a creation that sprung from his passion for improvisation.

When he received his diagnosis, he and Mel had just finished engineering a life that allowed her to stay home with their youngest of two children. Gabe had recently been diagnosed with autism, and Melanie couldn't make sense of working full-time to just barely cover their childcare expenses.

It certainly was a sacrifice to live solely off Nick's teacher's salary, but they made it work. Nick also taught private lessons, played gigs whenever he could, and led their church's music for extra cash and inspiration.

Stage 4 cancer is generally thought to be a terminal diagnosis. But Nick had enough drive and optimism to fuel hope for a recovery. A hope now deferred. A recovery that never came.

Walking into the church, I confess I just couldn't find the re-demptive story.

Nick's funeral was unique, a reflection of him. It was quirky, filled with music and humor. At Nick and Melanie's insistence, the funeral was dubbed a "Celebration of Nick's Life," but I was skeptical it could live up to such a billing.

Then came the testimonial section of the service, where friends, family, bandmates, students, and even members of a local mo-torcycle gang (it's a long story) waited in an endless line to share Nick's impact on their lives in the standing-room-only sanctuary.

Nick Selvi didn't leave much of an *estate*, but as I left his funeral, I couldn't help but think that he left more of a *legacy* in thirty-six years than most would leave in two lifetimes.

Simple Money Journal Entry

Legacy

I'm reminded of the three questions in chapter 2.

Do you see them differently through the lens of legacy?

And I invite you to consider three subsequent questions
I'm asking myself at the end of this chapter:

1. If today was my last day, what would my legacy be?
2. How would I like it to be different?
3. How would my goals (chap. 3) change if I viewed them as legacy-building opportunities?

Estate planning feels like a chore. It can be uncomfortable, time consuming, and expensive. I can certainly make the case that it is worth every discomfort, every moment and dollar spent, to draft the most important documents we may ever write. But when considering the opportunity it provides to pause—and consider our legacy—estate planning begins to feel more like a priceless gift.

Simple Money Estate Summary

---

1. Estate planning is the most important element of all financial planning because the damage done to one's plans for life and money without it can be catastrophic.

2. We don't like to do it, primarily because we'd rather avoid the topic (fear of death) and don't see it as urgent (because, really, what are the chances?).

3. The three essential estate planning documents, appropriate for most adults, are a will, durable power of attorney, and advance directives.

4. Watch out, because the wishes expressed in the beneficiary forms for your retirement accounts, annuities, and life insurance will trump the wishes in your will. Be sure they are in sync.

5. Your estate—the tangible stuff you collect throughout life—is important, but not as important as your legacy—the intangible, collective impact that you have on the world around you.

What INSIGHTS and ACTIONS did you take from this chapter?

PART 4

PLANNING
FOR THE
UNEXPECTED

*Avoid, reduce, and assume the risk
you can handle, and transfer the risk
that you can't with insurance.*

14

INSURANCE

WARNING!

WHY do I need to read this chapter?

You'll want to read this short chapter before buying any type of insurance because insurance products aren't the only way to manage risk. In fact, purchasing insurance—while entirely appropriate in many circumstances—should be the last resort in any risk-management strategy because it's the most expensive way to handle risk in the majority of cases.

Let's take just a few minutes to walk through the other three ways we can manage risk and then discuss how insurance actually works.

How to Manage Risk

There are four ways to manage any risk we might face. The first way is to *eliminate* the risk completely. John Madden, the famed football coach and commentator, was deathly afraid of flying. So he took the Madden Cruiser—a swanky bus—to all those *Monday*

Night Football games, even if they were cross-country trips. Of course, we know that flying is actually safer than driving, but we can't argue that Madden didn't successfully eliminate the risks associated with flying by simply not flying.

Next is a risk-management technique we use constantly, often without even noticing. It's risk *reduction*. We set an alarm clock to reduce the risk of being late to work. We wear a helmet to reduce the risk of being injured in a bike accident. We reduce the risk of overexposure to the sun by wearing sunscreen.

Third, we may *assume* risk, a risk-management technique perfected especially by teenage boys and young men. This is often the default risk-management decision for many, but don't doubt that it is a decision. When we enjoy the bliss of swimming in the ocean, we're assuming risks ranging from strong currents, wayward waves, jellyfish stings, and a one in 3,748,067[1] chance of a nibble from a shark.

The last way we manage risk is to *transfer* all or some of it to another party. When you hand someone your car keys, you're transferring risk. And any time you buy insurance, you do the same thing. You can insure just about anything you fear—from the loss of an iconic mustache[2] to the hazards associated with an asteroid impact. For this reason, it's imperative to understand that just because an insurance policy exists doesn't mean you should purchase it.

Eliminate. Reduce. Assume. Then, and only then, transfer risk.

A basic understanding of how insurance companies operate helps us understand why every risk shouldn't be transferred, and why it's foolish not to transfer others.

How Insurance Works

Insurance companies are in the pool-making business. Simply put, they take a group of people who share a common risk, but spread that risk across the entire collective or pool. Consider the example of an early life insurance "policy":

A primary occupation in colonial New England was commercial fishing. Recognizing the associated dangers, local churches would take up a collection each time sailors would go off to sea. In the event that one did not return, his family would receive the financial boost. The community shared in the risk.

The money we pay into an insurance policy—or an insurance pool—is called a *premium*. The money that exits the pool to compensate those who suffer a loss is called a *claim*. The organizer of the pool—the insurance company—receives the difference between the two, the profit. Therefore, the insurance company has an inherent conflict of interest. They prefer *not* to pay claims.

Premiums – Claims = Profit

If you're struggling to know whether a risk should be eliminated, reduced, assumed, or transferred, consider the Simple Money risk-management technique:

The Simple Money Risk Management Guide

1. Eliminate risks that offer little reward.
2. Reduce risks by employing common sense.
3. Assume risks that you can endure.
4. Insure catastrophic risks.

Contemplate this risk-management strategy in the light of the simple act of driving home from work:

1. Research suggests that texting while driving is *six times more dangerous*[3] than drunk driving. Most of us have done it at some point, but statistics such as these, and the stories of needless deaths, clearly indicate that the minuscule benefit to be gained from checking our email or sending a text in the 20 minutes it takes to commute home is simply not worth the risk. This is an easy one to eliminate completely.

2. Any time we step into a car, we know there's a risk of being involved in an automobile accident. But there are many decisions we can make to reduce the risk of that activity—most notably, wearing a seatbelt. After nearly losing my life in a car accident in which I did not wear a seatbelt (chap. 4), I'll never need to think twice about reducing this risk again.

3. Many of our insurance policies have a risk assumption feature built into them. It's called a *deductible*. That's the amount we're expected to pay out-of-pocket before the insurance kicks in. In the case of our driving-home-from-work scenario, most auto insurance agents recommend low deductibles—$50, $150, or $250. Of course, if we had a $500 claim—perhaps even a $1,000 fender bender—we're not likely to claim it through our insurance for fear of a lifetime of higher premiums. So, why pay for insurance that we don't want or plan to use when the alternative is a higher deductible that would lower our premiums?

4. The type of risk we should be happy to transfer is risk we simply couldn't assume ourselves. You can buy a new phone if you drop yours in the kitchen sink, but if you have an accident on the way home from work—and it's your fault, and the person you hurt sues you, and they win and are awarded a million bucks—chances are high that you couldn't write

that check. This particular type of risk can be transferred through a combination of your automobile insurance and your "umbrella" liability insurance—two types of coverage we'll discuss more in chapter 18.

The Simple Money risk-management method can be used effectively for every risk decision we make, from hitting the snooze button in the morning to shielding our families from the catastrophic financial risk associated with a tragic death—which happens to be the topic of our next chapter.

Simple Money Risk-Management Summary

1. There are four ways to manage risk—it can be eliminated, reduced, assumed, or transferred through the purchase of insurance. The last resort in any risk-management strategy should be the purchase of insurance, because it's the most expensive way to deal with risk.

2. Premiums are paid into insurance "pools," and claims are paid from those pools to people who suffer the risk they've insured against. The difference between the two is the insurance company's profit.

3. The Simple Money risk-management method:
   - Eliminate risks that offer little reward.
   - Reduce risks by employing common sense.
   - Assume risks that you can endure.
   - Insure catastrophic risks.

What INSIGHTS and ACTIONS did you take from this chapter?

15

LIFE

Harder Than It Needs to Be

WHY do I need to read this chapter?

The probability that you will die in this lifetime is high. *Really* high. The probability that you will die prior to retirement age is, however, quite low. As a non-smoking male at age 40, for example, I have only a 6 percent chance of dying prior to age 65.[1]

This low probability—in addition to our preference for generally avoiding the subject of our own demise—has a way of lulling us into inaction when it comes to life insurance, much as with estate planning (chap. 13). But, although the probability is low, the financial impact of death during your working years would likely be so significant that the topic deserves serious consideration. Estate documents can tell the money where to go, but life insurance creates the money where it is lacking.

Unless you are independently wealthy, if anyone relies on you financially, you likely need life insurance. The key is discerning what kind, how much, and how to buy it. Unfortunately, determining what's appropriate has been made much harder than it needs to be. But why?

214

Few financial planning topics are so strewn with information—information that often conflicts—as life insurance. This is, in large part, because of the myriad differences among life insurance products. And these differences are often driven by the compensation structure of insurance salespeople.

The good news, however, is that the coverage you likely need is simple and relatively inexpensive.

The Purpose of Life Insurance

Part of the reason life insurance is so confounding is that its purpose has been muddled. So let's simplify:

Life insurance helps compensate for the financial loss accompanying the loss of life.

This is not its primary purpose—it's the sole purpose.

Life insurance is not—I repeat, *not*—an investment. Some life insurance policies do have investment components, which we'll address, but there is almost always a better location for your investing dollars than in a life insurance policy. As Aaron Vickar, director of BAM Risk Management, said, "If you need insurance, buy insurance. If you want to invest, buy investments. Comingling the two is typically not in your best interest."

It's also important to note that the process we'll undertake to discern how much life insurance is appropriate for you is not an attempt to put a value on a human life. Instead, it is an attempt to arrive at the proper level of compensation for a household's economic loss due to the death of a loved one. This will be made clear especially when we're discussing how to accommodate for the passing of a stay-at-home spouse.

Few things in life are as difficult to endure as losing a loved one. The purpose of life insurance is to allow healing without the stress of financial strain.

I'd love to have a conversation about life insurance without industry jargon, but it's unavoidable, so I'll translate instead. First, individuals play three basic roles in a life insurance policy:

Simple Definitions

1. **The owner**—the person who pays the policy premiums.
2. **The insured**—the person on whose life the policy is based.
3. **The beneficiary**—the person who receives the death benefit.

The owner makes a contract with the insurance company—called a policy. As long as the owner continues to pay the policy premiums, the insurance company pledges to pay the beneficiary the death benefit if the insured passes away. So, when someone you know refers to having purchased a $1 million life insurance policy, the million bucks represents the death benefit.

Different Types of Life Insurance

Today there are two broad categories of life insurance: term and permanent. The fundamental difference is that term is constructed to shield policyholders from the financial risk of death for a stated period of time, while permanent is designed to go on interminably.

Although permanent insurance preceded term, it helps to explain the latter first. *Term life insurance* is, effectively, pure insurance. For a set period of time, as short as one year and typically no longer than thirty, an individual transfers the financial risk of death to the insurance company in exchange for the payment of a premium reflecting the probability of that individual's premature passing. Premature, or perhaps catastrophic, may be the operative word here, because neither term policies nor premiums are designed to protect one from naturally expected death.

Because *permanent life insurance* must be actuarially designed to be viable to the literal end—as opposed to term policies, which are intended to pay out only in unexpected catastrophic scenarios—the premiums must also be higher. And by higher, I mean substantially higher. Depending on the type of permanent insurance and the age and health of the insured, premiums for a policy with an identical death benefit could be five, ten, or even twenty times larger than a comparable term policy.

Another hallmark of permanent insurance is cash value, a savings mechanism that helps support a policy's performance over time and hopefully supplements a policy owner's other savings initiatives. A portion of each premium payment goes to support the insurance costs, while the balance is "invested" in the savings vehicle.

The differences among permanent policies, therefore, typically appear in the variations of savings mechanism. Here's a quick rundown.

Whole life insurance, the oldest surviving brand of life insurance, is, as you might anticipate, expected to last for one's whole life. The investing mechanism inside of a whole life policy is similar to that of a conservative fixed income vehicle, like US Treasuries or certificates of deposit (CDs). However, they are backed by the "full faith and credit" of the insurance company, not the federal government or the FDIC.

Typically the most costly of any life insurance product, whole life offers a policyholder the peace of mind that their policy will be there forever—as long as premiums are paid—and the savings mechanism will not be subject to stock market volatility.

Speaking of stock market volatility, the defining characteristic of *variable life insurance* is that policyholders *may* invest in the market through vehicles known as sub-accounts, the insurance world's answer to mutual funds.

Although the additional *expected* rate of return of such investment vehicles, relative to those found in whole life, should help reduce premium payments over the years, there are, of course, no guarantees that it will do so. It makes this particular type of life insurance, in my opinion, the least useful. If it is market investment you desire, I recommend you invest in the market, not in an insurance policy with an ancillary investment component.

The last variety of permanent life insurance you should be familiar with is *universal life*. Designed to be a less costly variety of permanent insurance, universal life is effectively a term/whole life hybrid. It is intended to last for a lifetime, but to do so in the most cost effective way possible. Therefore, it rarely amasses a significant amount of cash value. One quirky element found in universal life policies is that they can be very interest rate sensitive. Older policies created in high interest rate environments are notorious for requiring policyholders to actually increase their premiums if they want to keep the policy, now that interest rates are lower.

A Simple Money tenet is to avoid unnecessary complications in creating a financial plan. In most cases, that means avoiding permanent life insurance. The benefits rarely outweigh the complexity. Now, let's get out of the informational weeds and work our way toward the Simple Money Life Insurance Guide. In order to help make sense of our motivation behind buying life insurance, let's separate that motivation into two categories: needs and wants.

Life Insurance Needs

Life Insurance Needs answer the question, "What would need to be covered in the case of a death in the family?" Satisfying these needs would help ensure that a household continues to function financially even after the loss of someone who makes an economic contribution to it.

There are five primary life insurance needs:

1. Payment of final expenses
2. Repayment of debts and mortgages
3. Pre-funding expected educational expenses
4. Funding replacement of household duties
5. Replacement of lost income

Some of these needs are *immediate*, like the requirement to pay final expenses, such as those for a funeral and burial. No one wants to be thinking about money immediately following the loss of a loved one, so covering these expenses in advance provides a sliver of peace in the midst of personal upheaval.

Other life insurance needs are of a *mid-term* variety, like paying off debts and pre-funding the cost of education. Typically, these needs were funded, at least in part, by the decedent. Debts, mortgages, and the cost of education for minor children frequently represent the largest present and future financial household obligations. Relieving a surviving spouse of covering these responsibilities alone will help him or her get reestablished financially without the fear of looming bills.

Take note, business owners.

There is one life insurance need that applies only to you. In a case where there are two or more owners of a business, it is highly recommended that they have a "buy-sell" agreement. The purpose of this agreement is to lay out the plan for the company in the case that one of the owners dies. The agreement is then "funded" by life insurance, meaning it's used to create the available funds for the deceased partner to be bought out. If the venture is short term in nature, it could make sense to use a term policy. But if the business partners are lifers, it may make sense to use a permanent life insurance policy.

Still others are long-term needs, like re-creating a stream of income or compensating for the economic loss of someone who helped manage the household.

Simple Money Life Insurance Guide

Most forms of life insurance analysis involve high-effort attempts to capture every little detail about your life. The most common method is to apply an economic value to each of the life insurance needs, add them up, and then buy that much life insurance. But on my quest to simplify personal finance, a lingering question has persisted:

Why are we focusing on all these details when we could just use life insurance to replicate the income that a person brings into a household with a simple calculation? Is there an easier, simpler path that would apply to the vast majority of households?

Yes. Here it is:

Simple Money Life Insurance Guide

For income earners, multiply your annual income by 15. Then purchase a term life policy for as many years as you can conservatively expect to need the income.

Income x 15 = Life Insurance Need

For a stay-at-home spouse, purchase a policy with a death benefit of between $250,000 (if children are older) and $500,000 (if children are younger).

Why 15 times the individual's income? Primarily because it works. But know that it works for a reason. Most households use income for two basic purposes: to pay current living expenses, like a mortgage, and to save for future expenses, like college and retirement. Therefore, it's only logical that purchasing enough life insurance to reproduce the income lost would be sufficient.

It might even be superfluous to purchase enough insurance to pay off all debts, pre-fund education costs, *and* replace lost income. The only question remaining, then, is how much of a lump sum do we need, given that it's conservatively invested, to reproduce the income?

If we divide the annual income—say $100,000—by the amount of interest we could reasonably assume earning—say 5 percent (or .05)—that tells us how much money we'd need sitting in an account while earning five percent to generate $100,000 per year of income.[2] That brings us to $2 million, a multiple of 20. But, because life insurance is both science *and* art, we're allowed to acknowledge a couple of things:

1. While we're attempting to re-create a deceased person's income stream, the reality is that most households will move on. For example, a family might downsize their house. Many people will eventually remarry, rendering a large portion of the life insurance proceeds superfluous.

2. As coarse as it sounds to acknowledge it, household expenses will be less with one fewer member of the household.

Therefore, we can save some money on life insurance, which we hope to never use, by reducing our multiple from 20 to 15. It's the intersection of analysis and common sense.

In almost every life insurance need scenario, term life insurance would be the optimal risk transfer tool. Why? Because the need for life insurance should expire once the household is financially independent. Therefore, purchasing a life insurance policy with a death benefit that is 15 times the income of the person being insured for a term that lasts until the household will no longer need earned income should be sufficient.

Life Insurance Wants

Are there any other reasons for purchasing life insurance beyond these needs? Long ago, my sales manager at a large insurance company certainly thought so. He said, "Anyone who can fog a mirror is a life insurance prospect." While I couldn't disagree with him more, I'm happy to concede that there are valid reasons for *wanting* life insurance above and beyond one's needs, if you're willing to endure the inherent complication and cost:

1. Pre-insuring future needs
2. Creating an estate
3. Funding charitable bequests
4. Replacing an estate lost to taxes
5. Building cash value

Very few people make it into young adulthood without having a friend or acquaintance take up the trade of life insurance sales. But there aren't many older prospects who will allow themselves to be persuaded by a youngster. So, guess who just became their target prospect? You, or at least a younger you. Do you remember that awkward conversation?

Since you didn't have a spouse or children yet, there was very little evidence on which to base an argument for a life insurance need. But the newly minted agent said, "You're gonna need it eventually, what with all your impressive personal and professional potential." Plus, he says, "You're young now, so the insurance is cheaper."

While your potential was (and is) impressive, and while insurance is indeed cheaper when you're younger (and healthier), I'm hesitant to recommend insuring a risk until it becomes one. This, remember, is a general risk management principle: Avoid, reduce, and assume the risk you can handle and transfer the risk that you can't.

Perhaps you're nearer to the end of your saving days than the beginning, and while you don't have any dependents, you would like to leave an estate behind for heirs, loved ones, or a charity you supported during life. You may buy a life insurance policy for any of these purposes, thereby creating an estate that may not have otherwise existed. A noble want it may be, but it's surely not a need.

In my opinion, the most sensible—but least likely to be utilized—life insurance want is that of estate replacement. Those blessed to amass a net worth in excess of $5 million may expect the federal government to become an unintended beneficiary of their estates. The IRS collects a tax notoriously known as the "Death Tax" on estates north of $5.43 million (in 2015, indexed for inflation), although couples can safely shield twice that amount.

Now, you might think this a most glorious dilemma and feel no sympathy for these well-to-do. But what if I told you the federal estate tax is as high as 40 percent? That it often represents a third layer of taxation on these assets? That family businesses and farms can be forced to sell when liquid cash is not available to pay the estate tax? That the federal estate tax is a moving target, and until recently was applied to estates that were over $1 million at rates up to 55 percent? And that many *states* also have estate or inheritance taxes levied at varying thresholds and rates?

Okay, wealth replacement still may not constitute a life insurance need, but it's a valid want nonetheless. And it's a worthy consideration for those of significant means.

Lastly, we discuss the most common life insurance want—cash value. Cash value is the savings component associated with permanent life insurance. It builds over time and is available for withdrawal or borrowing during life, as a complement to the policy's death benefit. Sounds great, right? Yes, and it can be a useful financial tool. But it comes at a cost—five, ten, or even twenty times that of a comparable term policy.

Now, let's address the elephant in the room (not to be confused with the Elephant in chapter 3).

How to Buy Life Insurance

Into the Lion's Den

One of the oft-mentioned reasons I hear from folks balking at addressing their life insurance needs is that they don't want to deal with life insurance agents. But while there are still a number of agents who've earned the stereotype now applied to the entire industry, there are also many knowledgeable insurance specialists who do well by their clients. And frankly, I more blame the insurance industry proper—and its antiquated compensation regime—than the agents whose decisions often set them at odds with the clientele they serve.

Virtually all insurance agents are compensated by commission, which means they get a cut of the premium you pay to the insurance company. Typically, the commission will be between 50 percent and 100 percent of your policy's first-year premium.

It often surprises young, healthy, first-time life insurance shoppers to learn that a million-dollar term life insurance policy could be as inexpensive as $450 per year. Correspondingly, the agent's commission is also pretty low. But would you believe that the annual premium on a $250,000 whole life policy for that same healthy young person could be $2,000 or more—for only a quarter of the coverage? Because the commission would also be significantly higher, this means the agent has a greater conflict of interest. He or she is incentivized to sell the insurance policy that would leave the client woefully underinsured.

I wish this was a mere hypothetical example, but I've seen this play out too many times. Dave and Jen had three kids when I met them. What they needed was a $1.25 million policy on Dave's life and $500,000 on Jen, who worked part-time. What they owned was a single $250,000 whole life policy on Dave's life alone—that cost more than the two term policies they needed combined.

Because the motivation for selling permanent insurance products over their term counterparts is so significant, many marketing systems have been designed to twist reality in a way that compels the prospective buyer to view permanent insurance as a "no-brainer." One of the lines I've heard too many times is, "Buying term insurance is like renting—wouldn't you rather own your policy?" No, thanks—I'd rather *not* develop an unnatural emotional connection with my insurance policy, as I might my house.

Another classic: "Only 2 percent of term life insurance policies even pay out!" That's great news. I hope my term policy never pays out, because that means I'm still alive! Indeed, who would wish for their home to burn down so that they can receive the benefit from their homeowner's insurance policy? The point of insurance isn't to reap a payday but to transfer catastrophic risk that we cannot avoid, reduce, or self-insure until we are financially independent.

The best way to avoid getting caught in the middle of a gut-wrenching sales pitch that will make you question yourself is to know exactly how much and what kind of life insurance you want *before* interacting with an insurance agent. By all means, consider the agent's suggestions for slight variations on your plan, but remember that it's *your* plan, not theirs. If you've done the work ahead of time (the work you're doing right now as you read this), you should be able to confidently move forward without falling prey to a sales pitch.

A good starting place is one of several online resources for life insurance quotes. These will give you some idea of a reasonable price range after putting in minimal information. But after you've done so, I do recommend working with a real, live agent to complete your application process—not an 800 number or a faceless website. You're not likely to pay any more, and you'll get help navigating through the last step of the insurance purchasing process—underwriting.

Underwriting

Underwriting is the process through which insurance companies determine how much of a risk *you* are. The insurance company will subject you to a battery of questions private enough to make anyone blush. They'll ask about your personal health and habits, as well as that of your parents and siblings. If you're a full-time smoker or excess drinker, you can be prepared to pay two to three times as much for your life insurance. But if you enjoy a few cigars each year or a glass of wine at dinner, most insurers won't hold that against you.

The key is to answer these questions honestly but concisely. If telling the truth isn't motivation enough, getting busted in a lie could put a black mark on your insurability for all time. Companies actually review your medical records and take blood and urine samples. But that doesn't mean you should elaborate on all of your hopes and dreams. If they ask if you have plans to visit any dangerous foreign countries, don't delve into your future vision for building a Swiss Family Robinson–style tree house on the Amazon. If you don't have plane tickets, you don't have plans.

Navigating the underwriting process is reason enough for using an insurance agent. A good one will earn his or her pay.

How to Get Out of a Policy

Perhaps through this analysis you've learned that you no longer need life insurance that you already own. There are two primary reasons you might want to get out of, or end, an insurance policy:

1. *You don't need it.* Remember, once you've reached financial independence, you don't need life insurance anymore. If you own a term policy, getting out is extremely easy—you just

stop paying the premiums. Yup, that's it. When your premium is due, and you don't pay, you'll get a notice from the carrier, who will typically give you a couple chances to get back in. You can forestall these attempts by simply letting them know that you no longer need the policy.

2. *You don't want it.* Perhaps you are an example of the young parents who was sold $250,000 of whole life instead of the term insurance they needed? This family shouldn't just dump their life insurance immediately. They should apply for the appropriate coverage *first*—to ensure they survive the un-derwriting process—and then look into options for ending the unnecessary policy. If it's relatively new, the chances are good that you won't be walking away with any money, but at least you won't be paying exorbitant premiums anymore.

If, however, you own a permanent policy you've been pay-ing premiums into for many years, you should have some cash value built up. Especially if it's an older policy, the cash value may even be performing well as a supplementary investment. You can examine the policy's expected future performance by requesting an "in-force illustration." You may decide to keep the policy even if you don't need it. But if you intend to cash it in, you should also ask for a "cost basis report." If your cash value is higher than your cost basis, you may have a taxable gain to report.

Simple, but Not Easy

After you've done the work, financial planning for an unexpected death may be simple(r), but that doesn't mean it's easy. No, it's not always easy to discuss the personal and financial implications of our inevitable departure from this earth. But I find that when they are entered into with an open heart and mind, these conversations can be surprisingly life-giving.

Simple Money Life Insurance Summary

1. If anyone relies on you financially—unless you are independently wealthy—you likely need life insurance.

2. The good news is that the coverage you likely need is
   simple and relatively inexpensive. The bad news is that
   there is a ton of misinformation out there, making your
   life insurance decisions more challenging.

3. The purpose of life insurance is to help compensate for
   the financial loss accompanying the loss of life. That's it.
   Life insurance is not an investment.

4. Let's not overcomplicate matters. The *Simple Money Life
   Insurance Guide*: Purchase a term life insurance policy
   with a death benefit of 15 times your income for a term
   as long as you can reasonably expect your survivor to
   need the income.

5. It's not always easy to discuss the implications of our
   eventual demise, but healthy conversations on the topic
   can be surprisingly life-giving.

What INSIGHTS and ACTIONS
did you take from this chapter?

16

DISABILITY INCOME

Protecting Your Assets

WHY do I need to read this chapter?

You've got a machine sitting in the garage. It's a money-printing machine, and it's perfectly legal. This machine is expected to print $75,000 this year, before taxes. You'll use the net cash to pay your household expenses.

Each year, the machine will print 3 percent more than it did in the previous year, and it will continue doing so for the next 40. That means, over its lifetime, the machine will print $5,655,094.48,[1] easily making it your most valuable asset today. Yet it sits in your garage, between an inherited set of golf clubs and a wheelbarrow with a flat tire, unprotected. Uninsured.

The machine, of course, is you, or more specifically, your ability to generate an income. And it didn't come cheap. You and your parents invested years of training and likely tens of thousands of dollars in hopes that your machine would not only support you financially for a lifetime but launch another generation as well.

We don't question the need to buy insurance for the things our money machine purchases. But few know if—or at least how, and to what degree—their income generation engine is protected.

Do you?

You will by the end of this chapter.

Do You Really Need It?

The insurance product that helps protect your income in the case of a disabling injury is disability income insurance. Although, according to Carol Harnett, the president of the Council for Disability Awareness, it should be called "income protection insurance" because the focus on disability draws attention away from what is really being protected—your money-printing machine.

If you work for a medium- to large-sized company, you likely have a group disability income insurance policy as part of your benefits package. Indeed, you might have two—a short-term policy and long-term disability (LTD) coverage. But please don't stop reading here if you fall into that category. Unfortunately, you can't assume your group coverage is sufficient. Indeed, most group coverage isn't.

A short-term policy is helpful but isn't necessarily required to protect you from the risk it's designed to mitigate if you have saved adequate emergency cash reserves. The long-term policy, however, is the one on which we'll focus, because it deals with the far larger risk exposure.

Moving Parts

Disability income insurance policies contain a maddening number of moving parts. Here is a not-so-comprehensive list of provisions that can vary from policy to policy, but that you'll want to understand:

- *Base benefit*—This is the amount of income you'd receive monthly in the case of a qualifying disabling injury. Most policies (although not all) won't pledge a base benefit higher than 60 percent of your pre-disability income (after tax), lest policyholders become incentivized to conjure imagined disabilities.

- *Benefit period*—This is the maximum length of time for which your disability income insurance policy will pay benefits. A "lifetime" benefit typically extends only to age 65 or 67, the presumed retirement age.

- *Residual benefit*—This policy feature allows you to receive a portion of your benefit if you're capable of generating a portion of your income. Without the residual benefit, it may be an either/or proposition.

- *Elimination period*—This is the period beyond which your income-limiting disability must extend *before* you'll begin to receive a benefit (typically 30 to 90 days). The further you extend the elimination period, the lower your premium will be.

- *COLA*—Yes, there is a cost of living adjustment intended to help your LTD benefit keep pace with inflation, but for most policies, it kicks in only *after* the inception of your disability.

- *Future insurability options*—FIO enables you to purchase additional chunks of LTD coverage in the future. It's really the second half of what most of us would expect from a COLA provision. While this makes a ton of sense for insurance actuaries, it understandably feels like a "gotcha" for many consumers.

- *Renewability provision*—Another item that seems possible only in the land of insurance, renewability provisions stipulate whether or not, and to what degree, your insurance company could alter or cancel your coverage in the future.

- *Social Security offset*—There is a Social Security disability benefit, but it is notoriously difficult to qualify for. An offset provision will reduce your LTD insurance benefits by the amount of any Social Security disability benefit you happen to receive. Accepting the Social Security offset could reduce your premium without increasing your risk.

(Not) Flipping Burgers

Arguably, the most important provision in your LTD policy is the definition of the word *disability*. The primary distinction is whether your policy covers "own-occupation" or "any-occupation" disabilities.

An any-occupation policy requires that you be *un*able to perform the material duties of *any* occupation to receive your LTD benefit. Emphasis on *any*. With no offense intended to the lovely greeters at Walmart or the burger flippers of the world, we must acknowledge that the requisite skill required to perform the material duties of those jobs is quite limited. As is the pay.

Indeed, the whole point of disability income insurance is to help replace a portion of *your* income, not someone else's. Enter own-occupation coverage, and similar variants such as "modified own-occupation" and "income replacement." If you're disabled enough that you can't do *your* job, you're covered. That's the plan.

The only problem is that most group (employer) LTD policies are very limited in their application of the hair-splitting definition for what constitutes a disability. The vast majority of them read something like this:

Own-occupation for the first two years; any occupation to age 65.

This means that you're *reasonably* well covered for the first two years, but then, unless you've suffered a very serious disabling injury or illness, you're likely to lose your coverage. And even if you're still within the first two years, please note that you're likely not optimally covered for yet another drawback common among group policies—tax treatment.

Here's the problem. I mentioned earlier that the highest LTD benefit you're likely to receive from an insurance company is around 60 percent of your pre-disability income—after-tax. While 60 percent after-tax is still likely to be less than you received in your paycheck before your disability, especially when considering the likelihood of increased medical expenses during this time, it should hopefully be enough to float your household. And if you're paying for a private LTD policy with after-tax money, the benefit would be tax free. However, here comes the big "but."

If your company is deducting their payment of your group LTD premiums as a business expense—and most are—the benefit to you would be *taxable*. Yes, the IRS allows a tax break on only one end of this equation. This means your 60 percent disability income insurance benefit would really equate to more like 40 percent after tax, an amount that would almost surely result in a financial hardship for the majority of households.

These aren't the only limitations with most group policies. "Group LTD coverage generally ends when employment ends," says Zack Pace, senior vice president of benefits consulting at CBIZ Inc. Group policies generally aren't portable. And other common limitations, according to Pace, are exclusions for preexisting conditions, maximum monthly benefit caps (a big one for high-income earners), and no cost of living increase (which is especially limiting for younger workers).

What to do, then?

The Simple Money LTDi Guide

If you are one of the majority who has a watered-down group LTD plan and nothing else, consider the following plan of action:

The Simple Money LTDi Guide

1. *Analyze* your group plan, specifically the any/own occupation definitions and the benefit taxability.

2. *Lobby* your human resources department by suggesting the benefits of enhancing those provisions.

3. *Retain* a supplemental, private LTD policy through a reputable carrier with the following provisions and/or riders:

   a. *Base benefit* up to at least 60 percent of after-tax income. Higher, if available.

   b. *Benefit period* to age 65 would be great, but at least five years.

   c. *Residual benefit*, to ensure you can get a partial benefit if you work part-time.

   d. *Elimination period* of 90 days, or even 120 days if you can afford it.

   e. *COLA* so that your benefit will rise annually in the case of an extended disability.

   f. *Future insurability option* so that you can increase your base benefit with rising income (if this isn't included in the policy).

   g. *Renewability provision* to ensure you'll continue to be insured. Noncancellable/guaranteed-renewable is ideal.

   h. *Social Security offset* may complicate claims, but it will help save on premiums.

   i. *Disability definitions* might be the most important feature. "Any-occupation" is too weak, but pure "own-occupation" can be cost prohibitive. Consider "modified own-occupation," "income replacement," or the equivalent.

It's vital that you shop among only solid insurance carriers. "Carrier financial strength, ratings, and reputation" are some of the most important LTD policy considerations, according to Todd Grandy, a disability income specialist at Northwestern Mutual.

Disability Planning for the Self-Employed

We've spent the bulk of our time discussing how to enhance or supplement your disability income insurance if you're one of the majority of people who has a group disability income insurance policy through work. What if you're not? What if you work for a small company that doesn't offer LTD coverage at all, or you're self-employed?

Well, do you want the good news or the bad news first?

Okay, the bad. If you don't have any group coverage, you're going to have to spring for a long-term disability income insurance policy yourself. This is bad news because it's not particularly cheap. It is likely that covering up to 60 percent of your pretax income is decidedly more expensive than adequate life insurance, for example. But that's for good reason. Your chances of being disabled in your working years are significantly higher than your chances of dying—before age 65, anyway.

What could possibly be the good news, then? Well, if you're personalizing your policy instead of merely accepting what you get from your employer, you'll likely have much better coverage if you incorporate the provisions included in the Simple Money LTDi Guide.

If you are buying your own policy, however, it's important to remember what we discussed about taxes. Yes, if you're self-employed, you could deduct the premiums as a business expense, but that would require subjecting any benefits received to tax. Don't do it. Bite the bullet and pay your premiums (a smaller number) after-tax so that your benefits (a bigger number) will be tax free if needed.

Wheelchairs and Crutches

What's the first image that comes to mind when you read the word "disability"? For most, it's a wheelchair or something else that connotes a serious lack of physical functionality. But most disabling injuries aren't visible and only partially impair their victim's capabilities. Unfortunately, a partial disability can have a devastating impact on a household's finances as expenses, often medical, rise while income falls.

Although it's confusing, misunderstood, oversold, and underappreciated, long-term disability income insurance is for most income earners simply "the cost of doing business." Especially if you're in your thirties or forties and your future income is your largest asset. After all, you've got to protect that money-printing machine.

Simple Money Disability Summary

1. Your ability to produce an income is likely your biggest asset. It's like a money-printing machine. Properly insure that machine with disability income insurance.

2. Disability income insurance contains a maddening number of moving parts. Know which you need to pay attention to and which you can ignore.

3. The Simple Money LTDi Guide involves taking advantage of the best that your group policy at work has to offer and then getting a solid supplemental policy.

4. We tend to view disability as a total disability, and therefore underestimate the probability that it could happen to us. In reality, most disabilities are partial and invisible, but they can have a huge impact on our financial wherewithal.

What INSIGHTS and ACTIONS did you take from this chapter?

17

LONG-TERM CARE

When I'm Sixty-Four

WHY do I need to read this chapter?

In 1967, the Beatles released the song, "When I'm Sixty-Four." The lyrics are a preemptive plea to secure a relationship even when the realities of old age set in. Now, as the nation's largest generation whistles this tune into retirement, the question seems less rhetorical:

Who *is* going to take care of us in retirement?

Long-term healthcare is on the minds of retirees and pre-retirees, and for good reason. Rising healthcare costs don't appear to be slowing down. Employers, as well as local, state, and federal governments, are increasingly passing on the rising financial risks of healthcare to employees. And the most costly form of care, long-term healthcare, is not (I repeat, not) covered by Medicare.

Long-term care insurance (LTCi) would seem to be a ready solution, but it appears expensive and even more confusing than disability income insurance (chap. 16). Is long-term care insurance "the answer," or just a smoke-and-mirrors sales pitch? The answer lies somewhere in between, but this much is true:

While not everyone needs long-term care insurance, *everyone* needs a long-term healthcare plan.

Federal Programs

Before we get into long-term care insurance, let's discuss the programs that already are in place and into which most of us default:

In its own words, "Medicare is the federal health insurance program for people who are 65 or older, certain younger people with disabilities, and people with End-Stage Renal Disease (permanent kidney failure requiring dialysis or a transplant, sometimes called ESRD)."[1]

Although decisions involving Medicare are notoriously complex—the program is a veritable alphabet soup[2]—most of us are aware that Medicare is federally administered health insurance for retirees.

Within the context of this chapter, what Medicare does *not* cover—long-term care—is of greater importance than what it does. And just in case there is any ambiguity, let's define long-term care, again with a definition directly from Medicare:

> Services that include medical and non-medical care provided to people who are unable to perform basic activities of daily living like dressing or bathing. Long-term supports and services can be provided at home, in the community, in assisted living, or in nursing homes. Individuals may need long-term supports and services at any age. *Medicare and most health insurance plans don't pay for long-term care.* (my emphasis added)

It may be more precise to say that Medicare does not cover the costs of *longer* long-term care,[3] as the program will pick up the bill for select services (including hospice) so long as they do not extend beyond 100 days.

Many assume long-term care is administered by a nursing home, and while that belief is not false, it is incomplete. Long-term care is provided in numerous ways, including at assisted living facilities and in the home. What defines long-term care is one's need for help with ADLs (Activities of Daily Living), like bathing, dressing, transferring, toileting, continence, and eating. That's according to the Federal Long Term Care Insurance Program.[4]

While Medicare does not cover us for long-term care, Medicaid does:

> Medicaid is a joint federal and state program that helps with medical costs for some people with limited income and resources. Medicaid also offers benefits not normally covered by Medicare, like nursing home care and personal care services.

Unlike Medicare, Medicaid does help with the costs associated with long-term care, but it comes at a price—just about everything you own. Although some states differ, it is generally very difficult for an individual to qualify for long-term care coverage through Medicaid unless their net worth is below $2,000. That's not a misprint.

Medicaid is healthcare for the truly impoverished, at any age. While there are legal strategies people have employed to create the appearance of poverty (where it does not exist) for the purpose of qualifying for Medicaid, newer laws have made this more of a challenge.

Decisions, Decisions

So, we're all on our own to pay for long-term care. Or, we buy insurance—long-term care insurance. The decision we make depends largely on the answers to two questions:

1. What is the probability that you will need long-term care services?
2. Can you afford to self-insure, to fund it yourself?

Regarding the probability, the available numbers seem capable of indicating nearly anything. An oft-cited statistic promoted by the insurance contingent suggests that "more than 50 percent of us . . . will need some kind of long-term care."[5] But you can also find competing statistics,[6] which suggest the "more than 50 percent" stat is overblown.

Here's the problem: the only statistics that matter are those that will affect you and your family, and you won't know which ones those are until it's too late. As economist Richard Thaler, coauthor of the book *Nudge*, says, "No one thinks they need long-term care until two years after they need it."

So perhaps the more important question is the second. Can you afford to fund long-term healthcare if you end up needing it? According to the US Department of Health and Human Services, some average long-term care costs from the year 2010 are as follows:

- $205 per day or $6,235 per month for a semi-private room in a nursing home
- $229 per day or $6,965 per month for a private room in a nursing home
- $3,293 per month for care in an assisted living facility (for a one-bedroom unit)
- $21 per hour for a home health aide
- $19 per hour for homemaker services
- $67 per day for services in an adult day healthcare center[7]

So you tell me, could you afford an additional $80,000 or so of annual expenses (per person) following a long-term healthcare incident?

Perspective

Allow me to offer some perspective.

If your total net worth is less than $250,000, the cost of long-term care insurance is likely prohibitive, relative to the amount of assets being protected. In a comparatively short period of time, your assets would be consumed by healthcare costs and you could then rely on Medicaid to pick up the tab. On the other extreme, if your liquid net worth (excluding your home) is in excess of $2.5 million, you *may* consider yourself capable of self-insuring the long-term care risk, although I must disclaim that this is highly dependent on your non-health-related spending.

Does that leave you with the majority of Americans who fall within that vast, middle chasm? And therefore back to a conundrum?

Well, how about some additional perspective on the cost of long-term care insurance?

According to AARP, the average annual premium for a long-term care policy purchased by a person age 55 or younger, is $1,831. That's for a typical policy with reasonably good coverage. Per person. In 2012. If you're between ages 55 and 64, the number goes up to $2,261.[8] It only increases further from there. Unfortunately, these numbers also look a bit low in comparison to today's prices for similar ages and policies.

Is the decision looking any easier? I was afraid not. But I have some good news for you.

Solomonic Wisdom

Your choice need not solely be between two extremes—bearing all the financial risk of an extended long-term care stint or transferring all of that risk to an insurance company. You may recall from our risk management primer (chap. 14) that insurance is not the only—or in many cases, the preferable—way to manage risk. Before transferring the risk to an insurance company, we must consider ways we can eliminate, reduce, or responsibly assume it.

Therefore, if your financial situation appears strong, but not impenetrable, consider proportionately reducing the features of a bells-and-whistles LTC policy, and thereby, the premium. The irony here is that I rarely recommend the Cadillac policy to anyone. If you can easily afford the higher premiums, you likely have the sufficient means to warrant a smaller policy to begin with.

So here comes that hard part—understanding these policies.

Moving Pieces

I apologize in advance, but I've actually slimmed this list to address only the most important policy features. It's a simple accounting of moving pieces with accompanying explanations:

- *Facility daily benefit* is the cost *per day* (in most cases) the policy will cover. Consider acquiring quotes based on a policy that would cover you for $100 per day. Then you can easily determine a higher or lower multiple of that policy rate based on the round number.
- *Facility benefit period* is the length of time over which the policy will pay out. The average stay in a long-term care facility is between two and three years. Most people, however, utilize care for even less time. The numbers are skewed upward by the relative handful of folks who suffer from dementia or Alzheimer's disease for a particularly long stretch. If your tolerance for risk is very low, you may consider a lifetime benefit. But if you are focusing more on the probability, consider a five-year benefit.

- *Home care daily benefit* is the percentage of the policy benefit that could be applied to skilled care in your home. Because it's the preferred method for most people, you might only consider plans offering 100 percent of your benefit to be applied to home care.
- *Inflation protection* describes how the future inflation of healthcare costs will be factored into your benefit. With the future cost of healthcare expected to rise at a pace above the normal inflation rate, this should be a primary concern for the prospective insured. If you are in your fifties or sixties, strongly consider compound inflation protection. If you are in your seventies or older and considering a policy, the premiums are likely to already be extremely costly. You may consider a simple inflation protection calculation or no inflation protection to reduce the costs of the policy.
- *Facility elimination period* is the initial time frame in which the policy will not pay. Because Medicare will typically pay for the first 100 days, and because you hopefully have sufficient emergency reserves (chap. 7), consider an elimination period of 90 days or more.
- *Marital discount* is a meaningful price break for couples who are purchasing long-term care insurance (LTCi) together. Many insurance companies now offer "shared care" policies that offer less stringent underwriting and reduced costs. But be sure to consult your LTC plan before choosing this option. A couple should evaluate their health conditions separately. For example, a spouse with a family history of dementia or arthritis should strongly contemplate applying for LTCi before major symptoms occur, because by then, you're likely to be turned down.

The Simple Money LTCi Guide

The average policy prices mentioned above—ranging from $1,830 for someone under 55 to $2,260 for someone under 65—assumed that they provided a daily benefit of $150, four to five years of coverage *in home*, a 90-day waiting period, and 5 percent automatic compound inflation protection. The actual policy offers you receive will be dependent on current pricing, your geography, and especially, your personal health as determined through the underwriting process.

With that perspective, consider applying this guide for exploring your own coverage:

The Simple Money LTCi Guide

1. *Be honest* with yourself. When considering your age, health, lineage, retirement income, assets, and tolerance for risk in their entirety, is transferring all or a portion of your long-term care risk through insurance a wise move? (The default answer is "probably.")

2. *Get a quote* for long-term care insurance based on the following policy template:

   a. *Daily benefit* of $100

   b. *Benefit period* of five years

   c. *Home care benefit* of 100 percent

   d. *Elimination period* of 90 days

   e. *COLA* rider tied to inflation (CPI) if available

   f. *Marital discount* if appropriate

3. *Adjust the policy* to reflect your personal risk characteristics.

Since we used a round number for the benefit, $100 per day, it will be easy to discern how the policy premium would adjust in the event you change the coverage level, for example, a $150 or $180 daily benefit. In that case, the premiums would likely be about 50 and 80 percent higher, respectively. As with life insurance and disability income insurance, I recommend you seek the services of an insurance specialist to aid you in the process of acquiring a long-term care policy, as long as you've conducted this analysis and already know what you want.

The Bottom Line

I recognize that the bottom line—the annual cost of the policy—is a meaningful determinant of whether or not you will purchase this insurance. Unfortunately, too many people get sticker shock after being pitched a top-of-the-line policy, and ultimately purchase nothing. The Elephant has a gut feeling that this is important, but the Rider overrules (chap. 3), deeming such a policy cost prohibitive.

This is why I'll leave you with this highly technical advice, designed to synthesize the probability of your need for long-term care insurance with your tolerance for risk and willingness to part with premium dollars:

Something is better than nothing.

Simple Money Long-Term Care Summary

1. Who will take care of you if you need long-term healthcare in retirement? Not Medicare.

2. The probability of your need for long-term care insurance is likely exaggerated by the insurance industry, but it is still a risk that you can't ignore. Not everyone needs long-term care insurance, but everyone needs a long-term healthcare plan.

3. Be honest with yourself—could you afford an additional $80,000 per year (per person in your household) for a long-term healthcare incident?

4. If you have less than $250,000 in net worth, you likely should not buy long-term care insurance because the relative cost is prohibitive. If you have in excess of $2.5 million in liquid assets—not including your primary residence—you *may* consider self-insuring the risk of long-term care.

5. If you fall in the middle (and that's probably you), consider partially insuring the risk instead of ignoring it completely.

What INSIGHTS or ACTIONS did you take from this chapter?

18

HOME AND AUTO

Don't Overpay
to Be Underinsured

WHY do I need to read this chapter?

Of all the insurance products that are commonly bought and sold, home and auto insurance receive the least amount of scrutiny from buyers. Because we are required by law to have coverage if we own a house or vehicle, we tend to see these insurance products as pure commodities. This is why solicitations to save 15 percent in 15 minutes or to name our price actually work. Most people consider all home and auto insurance policies to be equal, as though price is the only consideration.

The end result is that most people are overpaying to be underinsured. Through the lens of the Simple Money risk management method, we can clearly see how to set our limits for home, auto, and the oft-forgotten "umbrella liability" coverage.

Auto

Let's start by looking at automobile insurance coverage, where I tend to see the most mistakes and, therefore, the biggest opportunities for improvement. The biggest mistake is having too little liability coverage, or in insurance parlance, "bodily injury liability" coverage. We began addressing this issue in our risk management primer in chapter 14.

Let's say you're driving home from work and you have an automobile accident. You weren't doing anything really dumb, like texting and driving, you just didn't brake soon enough and slammed into the car in front of you. Unfortunately, the person driving the car you hit was hurt and sued for damages—and won, awarded one million dollars. Who pays, and how much?

The answer is buried in your auto policy's "declaration pages," summarizing your coverage. Look at the numbers next to the label "bodily injury liability." It likely offers two numbers and reads something like $50,000/$100,000. Those numbers represent the amount that the insurance company will pay per person and per accident, respectively. So, in this case, since there was only one person in the car in front of you, of the million-dollar award, your insurance company would pay a total of $50,000. I hope you have an extra $950,000 lying around, because the rest is on you. In this example, you've covered a smaller risk and left yourself wide open to a massive, catastrophic financial risk.

Another number that often follows these first two—for example, $50,000/$100,000/$25,000—represents the amount of property coverage you have. As you might expect, this is the amount the insurance company will pay to repair any property that your at-fault accident might have caused. I don't need to tell you that it would be easy to do more than $25,000 worth of damage. Low limits here could put you on the hook yet again.

Another aspect of liability is hopefully in your auto policy—the "uninsured/underinsured" coverage. Often listed in the same fashion as your bodily injury liability coverage—like $50,000/$100,000—this policy component allows you to pay for the lacking coverage of someone with whom you have an accident. Maddening though it is to pay for coverage someone else neglected to acquire, this is an important piece of the auto insurance puzzle.

The second biggest mistake I see in auto policy structuring appears small—it's the size of your policy's deductible. The deductible is the risk assumption tool (chap. 14) that is built into most insurance policies. It is the amount you will pay out of pocket in the case of an accident, before the insurance company steps in. The lower your deductible, the higher your premiums. The higher your deductible, the lower your premiums.

Insurance agents are notorious for defaulting to very low deductibles, which works nicely in their favor—they receive outsized premiums in exchange for very little risk, especially since most drivers won't even place a small claim. Therefore, if (and only if) you have sufficient emergency reserves (chap. 7), you may lower your premium by raising your deductible. In fact, in many instances, I've seen drivers increase their catastrophic risk (by raising their liability limits) without increasing their overall premiums because they also increased their deductibles.

Typically, two different deductibles are mentioned on your auto policy—comprehensive and collision. Here's an easy way to remember which is which: The collision deductible is applicable when you have one—a collision. Comprehensive entails just about everything else—a tree falling on your car, hail denting your hood. Windshield repairs are the most common claim that falls under the comprehensive label, and some insurers actually have a separate deductible for those occurrences.

Home

Homeowner's insurance also has a liability feature that is no doubt underappreciated. Most policies are written with $300,000 of liability coverage. You might expect this to have an impact if one of the neighbor's kids falls on your sidewalk and the parents sue you (and it does), but guess what? Your homeowner's liability coverage actually follows you beyond the borders of your home. If you, like the legendary Chief Inspector Clouseau, accidentally destroy your neighbor's "priceless Steinway" piano, it may be *your* liability coverage (attached to *your* home) that pays the bill. (Of course, since Clouseau was on the job in his incident, it may well have been the French sûreté's policy that paid for the piano's repairs.)

When most of us think of our homes, we're actually thinking about our homestead—the house and the land on which it sits. But it's important to recognize that in most homeowner's insurance policies, it is specifically your *dwelling, other structures,* and *personal property* that are covered, not your land or landscaping. Coverage for your home is centered around the dwelling itself. The amount of coverage should be equivalent to what it would cost to rebuild the house from scratch if it burned to the ground, a complicating factor in the case of older homes with vintage molding or plaster walls. Other structures, like a detached garage, are typically covered for up to a certain percentage of the dwelling's value, an important consideration especially if you have a finished outbuilding.

Another important consideration for your homeowner's insurance is the coverage for the personal property within your home. "Full replacement value" is preferred over "actual cash value," and I highly recommend conducting a video inventory of the home's contents to ensure you get the full benefit of your coverage if it's ever needed. (Of course, be sure to keep the video *outside* of the home.) Also pay special attention to any policy limitations. For reasons that appear obvious, homeowner's policies replace items like cash, jewelry, and artwork only up to a limited amount ("Yes, I'm quite sure that it was $200,000 in cash that went up in flames.

Oh, and Van Gogh's 'Starry Night.' The original."). Additional coverage on these types of property often requires a specific policy supplement.

You can purchase additional coverage for most risks to your home, but please read the fine print, because there are some notable risks typically not covered by your basic homeowner's policy, according to Bankrate, such as a flood, mold, termite infestation, sewer backup, nuclear plant accidents, and most importantly, earth movement (such as an earthquake or sinkhole occurrence).[1]

Umbrella

As I mentioned in the chapter's open, most people have homeowner's and auto insurance because they are requirements of owning a home or automobile. This next type of insurance is missed by nearly everyone—because it's not required—but it is one of the best Simple Money risk management tools, the excess liability "umbrella" policy.

You may recall the conundrum we had with low personal injury liability limits in auto insurance—if you had only $50,000 of liability coverage and were sued successfully for a million bucks, you'd be on the hook for $950,000. You might think the ideal alternative is simply to raise your auto liability coverage to $1,000,000, but most insurers will only allow you to increase your limits to $250,000 or $500,000. Similarly, you may want more than $300,000 of personal liability coverage attached to your home.

What is going to make up the difference? *Excess liability* coverage acts as an umbrella layer over your home and auto insurance, boosting your liability limits on either of those underlying policies if needed. The good news is that this coverage catapults you from being underinsured to adequately insured. The great news is that it's surprisingly inexpensive. A typical household's excess liability coverage will only cost between $150 and $250 *per year*, and may even result in reduced premiums for your underlying home and auto policies.

Interestingly enough, because the premiums on umbrella policies are relatively low but the claims, however rare, can be high, I've found that some insurance agents actually *under*sell umbrella policies. After all, if a claim hits, it can be bad for profit (chap. 14). So, if your agent tries to talk you out of an umbrella, that's a good sign that he is looking out more for himself than you—time for a new agent.

Simple Money Home and Auto Guide

Looking for guidance on your home and auto insurance? Look no further, but please be sure to take into account factors that are unique to you and your geography:

Simple Money Home and Auto Guide*

Automobile Insurance Limits	
Bodily Injury Liability:	$250,000 per person
	$500,000 per accident
Property:	$250,000
Uninsured/Underinsured:	$250,000/$500,000/$250,000
Comprehensive Deductible:	$500–$1,000**
Homeowner's Insurance Limits	
Dwelling:	Replacement Value
Liability:	$300,000
Earthquake/Land Movement:	Yes
Deductible:	$1,000–$2,000**
Excess Liability Limits	
Umbrella:	$1,000,000 up to Net Worth

*The figures offered are generalizations and should be used only as a guide.
**Higher deductibles are appropriate only when the result is meaningfully lower premiums and you have sufficient emergency reserves.

Simple Money Home and Auto Summary

1. Home and auto insurance receives the least scrutiny from buyers because it's such a commoditized product. The result is that most people are overpaying to be underinsured.

2. The biggest hole in most home and auto insurance is lacking liability coverage, a hole that can be covered by increased liability limits and an "umbrella" policy. The increase in premiums may then be offset by increasing deductibles, but only if you have sufficient emergency reserves.

What INSIGHTS and ACTIONS did you take from this chapter?

PART 5

PLANNING FOR ACTION

The best plan in the world is worthless until it is put into action.

19

THE TOP 10

Your Next Dollar's Home

WHY do I need to read this chapter?

No matter how much money you have or make, it could never keep up with all the seemingly urgent invitations to part with it. My hope, therefore, is that by offering a suggested path of financial priorities, you might use this list to finalize your own.

Separating true financial priorities from flash impulses is an increasing challenge, even when you're trying to do the right thing with your money—like saving for the future, insuring against catastrophic risks, and otherwise improving your financial standing. And while every individual and household is in some way unique, the following list of financial priorities for your next available dollar is a reliable guide for those in search of direction.

Once you've spent the money necessary to cover your fixed and variable living expenses (and yes, I realize that's no easy task for many), consider spending your additional dollars in the order on the following pages.

Top 10

1. *Create (or update) your estate planning documents.* Your estate planning, or lack thereof, is unlikely to make headlines like the financial missteps of the rich and famous. But the frightening implications of not planning for your inevitable demise lands it in the top financial priority slot, especially for parents of minor children. With rare exceptions, every independent adult should have the following three documents drafted, preferably by an estate planning attorney: a will, durable powers of attorney, and advance directives (healthcare power of attorney and a living will).

2. *Ensure that insurance needs are met.* Don't become the next heart-wrenching *20/20* segment because your family was left destitute after you died or became disabled without adequate insurance for such a catastrophic event. Please note, however, the difference between insurance needs and wants (chap. 15). Surprisingly, most insurance needs—especially regarding life insurance—are sufficiently covered with policies that are less expensive than the all-inclusive, bell-and-whistle products often recommended by insurance agents.

3. *Pay off any high-interest consumer debt.* It's hard to build assets when you're dragged down by liabilities. A new report out from the Urban Institute indicates that one in three Americans have debt in *collections*.[1] You know, collections—when you get nasty calls from unforgiving call centers that purchased your debt for pennies on the dollar from credit card companies and medical care providers, among others. That's approximately 77 million people! The economic and emotional toll of consumer debt, especially at astronomical interest rates, makes it financial enemy number one (or, in this case, number three).

4. *Build at least one month's worth of living expenses in emergency savings.* Savings are the first line of defense against cancerous consumer debt. Yes, of course I'd like you to have more than a month of expenses saved, but the next priority is just too good to put off.

5. *Earn free money by taking advantage of your company's 401(k) match.* Many companies offer to incentivize employee retirement savings by matching, up to a certain amount, the percentage of your salary that you contribute to the company retirement plan. They may match 100 percent of the first 3 percent of the salary you elect to defer, or 50 percent of the first 6 percent. In any case, give yourself a guaranteed rate of return by gobbling up those matching contributions from your employer. If not, you're leaving money on the table. It's all I can do to keep from making this number one!

6. *Contribute to a 529 plan for education savings.* Education should not be prioritized over retirement, and merely contributing the matched amount to your 401(k) is not likely to secure your post-work future. But once you have checked off numbers one through five, it's time to consider opening up 529 accounts for children you intend to help through college. Contribute what you can and invite loving relatives to do the same.

7. *Contribute the maximum possible to your Roth IRA(s) if your income level allows you to.* Nothing's better than free money, but tax-free money comes close. By contributing to a Roth IRA, you're filling a bucket of money that should never be taxed (as long as you wait until after age 59.5 to take gains). And, if you are hit with an emergency that runs through your reserves, you can take your principal contributions back out of your Roth IRA at *any* age for *any* reason without taxes or penalties. In 2015, you can contribute

$5,500 per person or $6,500 per person if you're age 50 or older. The ability to contribute to a Roth IRA goes away entirely, however, if your income level is above $193,000 in 2015.

8. *Return to strengthen your emergency reserves, offering sleep-at-night peace.* I like to see most households with stable jobs amass three months of reserves, households with more volatile income sources put away six months of savings, and the self-employed stockpile a year's worth of expenses. Sounds like a crazy sacrifice, but what better to spend your money on than peace of mind?

9. *Come back to your 401(k) and cap it off.* If you still have money left after taking advantage of numbers one through eight, you probably have a fairly high income. Maxing out your 401(k) or other corporate retirement plan will not only further pad your retirement savings but will also reduce your taxable income for every dollar contributed. You may contribute up to $17,500 per person—and a whopping $23,000 for investors 50 or older—in 2015.

10. *Set aside excess savings in a liquid, taxable investment account for midterm needs and projects.* Emergency savings helps protect you in the short term. 401(k) and Roth IRA investments help secure your financial future. But if you're only taking care of the short and long term, it leaves nothing for the midterm. Therefore, opening a regular, taxable investment account will help you set aside money for excess education costs, a closely held business investment, the down payment on a second home or rental property, or a boat (the most glorious way to flush money down the head). This money should be invested in accordance with the time horizon for its use.

Purposefully Excluded

Conspicuously missing from this list are nondeductible Traditional IRAs, annuities, all forms of permanent life insurance, and hundreds of other marketed repositories for your money. These products may have their uses, but they simply don't take priority over these ten financial imperatives.

In all, I estimate the "cost" of checking off each of the listed priorities to be more than $70,000 annually, surely requiring combined household income of $250,000 or more. Impossible? That's not the point. The point is you can likely free yourself from worry about any of the additional pitches that come your way until you've mastered each of these ten financial priorities. Rejoice in the good news that you can vastly simplify your financial planning by ignoring most of the personal finance noise that is cluttering your decision-making.

Simple Money Summary

Once you've spent the money necessary to cover your fixed and variable living expenses, consider spending your additional dollars in this order:

1. Create (or update) your estate planning documents.
2. Ensure that your insurance needs are met.
3. Pay off any high-interest consumer debt.
4. Build at least one month's worth of living expenses in emergency savings.
5. Earn free money by taking advantage of your company's 401(k) match.
6. Contribute to a 529 plan for education savings.
7. Contribute the maximum possible to your Roth IRA(s) if your income level allows you.

8. Return to strengthen your emergency reserves.

9. Come back to your 401(k) and max it out.

10. Set aside excess savings in a liquid, taxable investment account for midterm needs and projects.

What INSIGHTS or ACTIONS did you take from this chapter?

20

BEHAVIOR MANAGEMENT

Working with an Advisor

WHY do I need to read this chapter?

If personal finance was merely the study of money within the context of life, then all you'd need to do is act on the wisdom of the many experts represented in this book (and elsewhere) and be on your way. But as we learned in chapter 1, personal finance is more personal than it is finance. It's actually the study of life within the context of money.

Personal finance is more about behavior management than money management. That's why I, and many other financial advisors, actually have our own financial advisors. Yes, a great advisor may tell us something we aren't aware of, but more often than not, they'll simply remind us of what we already know and nudge us in the right direction.

The challenge, for you as a consumer, is finding a true advisor. Someone who is a practitioner of a trade, not merely a salesperson. Someone who is educated, credentialed, and experienced. Someone who acts in your best interest at all times.

Would you believe that the majority of financial services professionals are not legally obligated to act in your best interest at all times? Indeed, many of the most recognizable companies, firms that often represent the financial industry as a whole in the minds of many investors, have fought hard to keep their employees from having to make such a pledge.

Please allow me to help you decipher whether you're working with a salesperson or a professional. In order to do so, you need to know both how advisors are compensated and a bit about how they are regulated.

How Advisors Are Compensated

Three primary compensation methods drive the industry—commission-only, fee-only, and fee-based. What you'll find is that an advisor's compensation model drives his or her recommendations. And too often, the Elephant squashes the Rider (chap. 3).

The first, and at one time the only, compensation regime in the financial industry was the commission model. In this model, a stock broker or insurance agent would sell a stock, bond, mutual fund, annuity, or insurance policy and receive a commission, typically a cut of your initial investment or premium payment. The driving force of the client interaction between commission-based financial professionals and their customers was not advice but transactions. That was the only way the "advisor" got paid.

Commissions for the sale of products are still alive and well today. This is in part because the majority of financial services professionals work for the very companies that create the investment, insurance, and banking products. This isn't tolerated in other professions, like medicine (thankfully). Would you, after all, seek the advice of a doctor employed by a pharmaceutical company? Would you question the prescription written for you if you knew the physician was paid more to prescribe that medication over others? But this is still how many in the financial industry are compensated.

On the other end of the compensation continuum, we have fee-only advisors, who are compensated only by their clients. Even within this camp, there are numerous ways a client might pay an advisor. Some advisors charge on an hourly basis, like an accountant. Others charge a retainer, like an attorney. But most fee-only advisors charge clients based on the amount of assets they help manage, where the financial planning and investment fees are combined.

I much prefer fees to commissions. It places the advisor on the same side as the client, not a financial product. This compensation model, however, still isn't perfect. Hourly advisors have an incentive to stretch meetings or engagements, retainer or flat-fee advisors have an incentive to spend the least time possible on each client, and advisors who are compensated by "assets under management" are incentivized to keep as much as possible of their clients' net worth under management, where they can charge a fee.

The third compensation method is currently the most popular—fee-based. The biggest problem with this compensation label is its ambiguity. As it connotes, an advisor receives some of his or her compensation from fees, and some from commissions. It's hard to know exactly where the conflicts of interest are when you don't know exactly how the advisor is getting paid, which leads me to a very important point.

The ideal situation calls for no conflict of interest between client and advisor, but the best we're able to achieve in reality is low conflict. Everyone is biased in any circumstance where they have a financial stake in another's decision. Doctors, lawyers, educators, pastors, and plumbers—each have a conflict of interest. The goal is to ensure that all parties fully disclose their conflicts and limit them to the greatest degree possible. That's where regulators come in. And while the next section certainly may not be the most exciting in the book, I implore that it might be one of the more important.

How Advisors Are Regulated

Because of conflict abuse, regulatory bodies have sprung up to create legal standards by which financial professionals operate.

The lowest level of care is the same standard used by the local big box store—*caveat emptor*, or buyer beware. While insurance products are regulated by each state, most insurance policies and fixed (as well as indexed) annuities are sold on this primitive basis. It's *your* responsibility—not the agent's—to determine whether or not a product is right for you. The agent is representing the product. The exclusion in the insurance world is for products that have the label "variable." Variable life insurance and annuity products require that the selling agent step up one notch to the brokerage industry's standard—suitability.

The *suitability* standard requires every broker transacting in stocks, bonds, mutual funds, or any other security regulated by FINRA (the Financial Industry Regulatory Authority) to sell only products that could reasonably be considered suitable for the client at the time of sale. According to Barbara Roper, the director of investor protection at the Consumer Federation of America, "You can satisfy the suitability standard by recommending the least suitable of the suitable options, as long as it falls within the general suitability test. And you don't have to disclose your conflicts of interest."[1] She continues, "You don't have to appropriately manage your conflicts of interest or minimize your conflicts of interest."[2]

Sounds reassuring, doesn't it?

The highest standard—the *fiduciary* standard—was established by yet another regulating body, the SEC. The Securities and Exchange Commission was created as part of the Investment Advisors Act of 1940, in the wake of the financial destruction of the Great Depression. A fiduciary must place his or her interest after that of the client's. Clients have to be put first.

Why doesn't everyone holding themselves out as some sort of financial professional, consultant, planner, specialist, or advisor have to act in the best interest of his or her clients? That's a great question to ask your prospective advisor. How are you compensated and how are you regulated? Which hat are you wearing?

If the individual is truly operating in a fee-only capacity, they must be acting as a fiduciary. But keep in mind that someone who sells only life insurance and fixed annuities is likely wearing only the *caveat emptor* hat, while someone who sells only variable insurance products and market securities is probably wearing the suitability hat. What makes the fee-based realm especially complex, from a regulatory perspective, is that someone might be acting as a fiduciary advisor at one moment, a suitability broker the next, and then a *caveat emptor* salesperson—all in the very same meeting.

Now, let's be clear. Just because someone is held to a fiduciary standard doesn't mean he's a fiduciary in principle. (I know some of those.) Conversely, someone who only sells insurance, while not held to a fiduciary standard, may be a genuine fiduciary, in the non-legal sense, through and through. (I know some of those as well.)

That said, if you had an opportunity to work with one of three advisors—and each had the same level of experience, education, and expertise—but only one of them was wearing the fiduciary hat, who would you pick? Well, I can assure you that you have this choice, if you know how to look.

Minimum Requirements for an Advisor

When you hire a financial advisor, you're the boss. So I recommend applying these minimum requirements in your search:

> Your advisor should be an experienced fiduciary who provides evidence of expertise in a field in which they are educated and credentialed.

I Hope . . .

Those are minimum requirements, but you deserve better.

Specifically, don't expect anything less than a planner who listens more than they talk, who puts you at the center of their universe in every conversation, and who will place themselves in your shoes to understand your values and priorities, your goals, and your calling.

And why stop there?

I hope you also find an advisor who encourages you to maintain a healthy level of cash and who helps you along your path to being debt free.

I hope your advisor is part of the newer school of investors who construct portfolios based on evidence (not opinion) and create asset allocations based on your willingness, ability, and need to take risk.

I hope your advisor has a broader view of retirement—that is, financial independence—and is comfortable helping you engineer Act Two of your three-act play.

I hope your advisor sees insurance decisions through the lens of risk management, helping you eliminate, reduce, and assume risk before you transfer it, and only then through the most cost-effective measures.

I hope your advisor will help you find the best home for your next dollar, even if it means not making a commission *or* accepting a fee.

But most of all, I hope you understand that no advisor, productivity system, app, investment, job, insurance product, financial plan, or book can give you what you really need. All those things are only vehicles on your road to Enough. The final vehicle we'll explore is designed to truly simplify all the work you've done to this point in a summary financial plan consisting of only a single piece of paper.

Simple Money Advisor Summary

1. Because personal finance is more personal than it is finance, a financial advisor is needed more for behavior management than money management.

2. There are three primary compensation models for advisors—commission-only, fee-only, and fee-based. Each of them has their own biases, but fee-only advisors offer the least conflicts of interest.

3. There are three primary regulatory models—insurance agents operate under a *caveat emptor* (buyer beware) standard, investment brokers operate under a suitability standard, and registered investment advisors (RIAs) operate under a fiduciary standard. Only the fiduciary is obligated to act at all times in the best interest of their clients.

4. The *minimum* requirements for any financial advisor you hire: Your advisor should be an experienced fiduciary who provides evidence of expertise in a field in which they are educated and credentialed.

What INSIGHTS and ACTIONS did you take from this chapter?

21

SIMPLICITY

The One-Page Financial Plan

WHY do I need to read this chapter?

Hopefully, our journey through and past complexity has brought you to a place where some very important decisions have become clearer, simpler. In this chapter, I offer a strategy that will help ensure this is the case.

A Sharpie and Some Card Stock

I have seen—heck, I've created—financial plans more than a hundred pages long. It was a mistake, and if one of those plans was yours, I apologize.

My friend, colleague, and *New York Times* contributor, Carl Richards, has helped me fully appreciate that financial planning is a process, not a product. Hitting a client with everything at once can be counterproductive for several reasons, but primarily because it's overwhelming. We wilt under the pressure and more often accomplish nothing than we do everything.

Richards developed a solution that sprang from his own family's financial awareness—the *One-Page Financial Plan*, now a book of the same name. Carl and his wife sat down with a Sharpie and a single page of card stock, forcing an element of brevity.

At the top of the one-pager, they wrote down a statement of their values followed by three goals—only three. They limited themselves to action required to work toward those goals, right now. That was it.

Pulling It All Together

I wholeheartedly endorse this strategy and offer a one-page *Simple Money* method. At the top of a sheet of paper, write "One-Page Financial Plan." Then turn it over and use the back as a worksheet:

1. *Compile your Insights and Actions.* The wisdom of the one-page plan is that you can't do it all at once. Financial planning is a perpetual process, not a one-time exercise. But at the same time, creating a receptacle for information we want to remember frees us to use our brain space for other pursuits (and thereby reduces our stress). Hopefully you've been aggregating your Insights and Actions from *Simple Money* in the online tool available at www.simplemoney.net/tools or in your own journal. If not, take a few moments to compile the notes and highlights now, just to be sure nothing slips through the cracks.

Simple Money Insights and Actions

Insights	Actions

Insights	Actions

2. Then, on the other side of that sheet of paper, *draft your one-page financial plan.* At the top, list the limited number of priorities in life that we worked on in chapter 2. Follow that with the self-selected, authentic, and others-oriented goals we generated in chapter 3. Finally, list only a handful of the next actions you intend to take at this time to work toward those goals. (See the example below and use it as a template if you're inclined.)

Simple Money One-Page Financial Plan

Priorities:

1. _____

2. _____

3. _____

4. _____

5. _____

6. _____

7. _____

Goals:

_____

_____

_____

_____

_____

_____

Next Actions:

☐ _____

☐ _____

☐ _____

☐ _____

☐ _____

☐ _____

Your one-page plan is a living, breathing document to be re-visited at least annually, preferably in a comfortable environment. It only expects of you what you can reasonably do now. If this book has revealed a number of actions you'd like to take, please remember that you have only so much time and you can stretch your dollars only so far. If you need help prioritizing your next actions, revisit chapter 19, "The Top 10: Your Next Dollar's Home."

I do believe that, by dedicating yourself to the guidance in *Simple Money*, you can dramatically improve your financial standing. And I hope you do. But most importantly, I pray you see money as it really is: a simple tool that can be used to navigate life's complexity on your path to Enough.

ACKNOWLEDGMENTS

Many thanks.

To my wife, Andrea, and my sons, Kieran and Connor, for emboldening me in my absence and enduring me in my presence, especially when a deadline is looming.

To Adam Birenbaum, Dave Levin, Al Sears, Jeff Remming, Mont Levy, Stuart Zimmerman, and Bert Schweizer, for trusting me with a message far weightier than my voice alone can support, and to Larry Swedroe, Kevin Grogan, and Jared Kizer, for educating me and helping ensure the veracity of my guidance. To Meredith Boggess, for fueling me with encouragement, and to Nick Ledden, for refining every word I write.

To Carl Richards, Sharon Epperson, Jim Pavia, George Mannes, Jean Chatzky, Manisha Thakor, and Ron Lieber, for inspiring me with their excellence and shaping my work.

To Jim Myers, Susan Engle, Kelli Lanfersieck, Patrick Akins, Ken Rosenbaum, and Joe Goldberg, for linking arms with me and pointing my energy in the right direction.

To Greg Johnson, my agent and guide, as well as Rebekah Guzman, Barb Barnes, Ruth Anderson, Janet Kraima, and the entire team at Baker Books, who have consistently exceeded my expectations.

And especially to Robin Maurer, who will always be my foremost editor, and Jim Maurer, who will always be my biggest fan.

NOTES

START HERE

1. Simon Sinek, "How Great Leaders Inspire Action," TEDx Puget Sound, September 2009, http://www.ted.com/talks/simon_sinek_how_great_leaders_in spire_action?language=en.

Chapter 1 Enough

1. John D. Rockefeller, *John D. Rockefeller on Making Money* (New York: Skyhorse Publishing, 2015).

2. John D. Rockefeller Sr., quoted in Ron Chernow, *Titan: The Life of John D. Rockefeller, Sr.* (New York: Vintage Books, 2004), 189.

3. Carl O'Donnell, "The Rockefellers: The Legacy of History's Richest Man," Forbes.com, June 11, 2014, http://www.forbes.com/sites/carlodonnell/2014/07/11/the-rockefellers-the-legacy-of-historys-richest-man/.

4. Daniel Kahneman, *Thinking, Fast and Slow* (New York: Farrar, Straus, and Giroux, 2011).

5. Brad Klontz, Ted Klontz, and Rick Kahler, *Wired for Wealth* (Deerfield Beach, FL: Health Communications, Inc., 2008).

6. Pablos S. Torre, "How [and Why] Athletes Go Broke," *Sports Illustrated*, March 23, 2009, http://www.si.com/vault/2009/03/23/105789480/how-and-why-athletes-go-broke.

7. James A. Finley, "What Could Happen to You: Tales of Big Lottery Winners," AP, Friday, May 17, 2013, http://usnews.nbcnews.com/_news/2013/05/17/18323470-what-could-happen-to-you-tales-of-big-lottery-winners.

8. Susan Bradley with Mary Martin, *Sudden Money: Managing a Financial Windfall* (New York: Wiley, 2000).

9. Susan Bradley, quoted in Moira Somers, "Advising Clients with Painful Money Legacies," September 24, 2014, http://www.suddenmoney.com/index.cfm?fuseaction=blog.details&ArticleId=22.

10. Byron Katie with Steven Mitchell, *Loving What Is: Four Questions That Can Change Your Life* (New York: Harmony Books, 2002).

11. This number is actually down quite substantially thanks to an infusion of cash from the Spanish government, fueling a plan to transform the dump into a landfill and displace the residents of La Chureca. Unfortunately, this has actually increased the desperation of the remaining residents as their source of sustenance has dwindled in size. Additionally, most of the major cities in Nicaragua have a similar dump with a similar population.

12. El Colegio de la Esperanza, (the School of Hope).

Chapter 2 Values

1. Benjamin Franklin, *The Autobiography of Benjamin Franklin* (New York: Touchstone, 2004), 67–68.

2. Ibid., 66.

3. Ibid., 72.

4. Ibid., 74–75, italics in original.

5. Claire Díaz-Ortiz, "What a Dreamboard Can Do for You," http://clairediazortiz.com/why-you-need-a-dream-board/.

Chapter 3 Riding the Elephant

1. Daniel H. Pink, *Drive* (New York: Riverhead Books, 2011).

2. Ibid.

3. Jonathan Haidt, *The Happiness Hypothesis* (New York: Basic Books, 2006).

4. Chip Heath and Dan Heath, *Switch: How to Change Things When Change Is Hard* (New York: Broadway Books, 2010).

5. Ibid.

6. TD Times Staff, "How Is a Next Action List Different from a To Do List?" February 10, 2011, www.gettingthingsdone.com/2011/02/how-is-a-next-action-list-different-from-a-to-do-list/.

Chapter 4 Calling

1. Os Guinness, *The Call: Finding and Fulfilling the Central Purpose of Your Life* (Nasvhille: W Publishing Group, 2003), 4.

Chapter 5 Time

1. Ryan Carson, "7 Do's and Don'ts for Founders," *The Naïve Optimist*, http://ryancarson.com/post/25580650719/7-dos-and-donts-for-founders.

2. Ibid.

3. Claire Diaz-Ortiz, "When Is the Best Time to Respond to Emails?" http://clairediazortiz.com/best-time-to-respond-to-emails/.

Chapter 6 Perspective

1. Andrea Coombes, "Retirement Savings: How Much Is Enough?" Market-Watch, February 16, 2013, http://www.marketwatch.com/story/retirement-savi ngs-how-much-is-enough-2012-09-12.

2. Ibid.

Chapter 7 Essentials

1. Bill Fay, "Demographics of Debt," Debt.org, http://www.debt.org/faqs/americans-in-debt/demographics/.

2. A standard ARM has an interest rate that adjusts with prevailing interest rates, but the **option** ARM actually allowed the borrower to choose their mortgage *payment* and also allowed that payment to be low enough that the mortgage balance would *increase* instead of decrease. The commission for these products was *double* the typical mortgage commission.

3. "Mortgage Payoff Calculator," Bankrate, http://www.bankrate.com/calculators /mortgages/mortgage-loan-payoff-calculator.aspx.

4. Tim Chen, "American Household Credit Card Debt Statistics: 2014," nerd-wallet, http://www.nerdwallet.com/blog/credit-card-data/average-credit-card-d ebt-household/.

5. "Credit Card Calculator," Bankrate, http://www.bankrate.com/calculators/ managing-debt/minimum-payment-calculator.aspx.

Chapter 8 Financial Statements

1. One-time $60 fee, as of May 5, 2015.

2. Rick Kahler, *The Financial Wisdom of Ebenezer Scrooge* (Deerfield Beach, FL: Health Communications, 2006), 3.

Chapter 9 Investing

1. Brian Wimmer, CFA, Sandeep Chhabra and Daniel Wallick, "The Bumpy Road to Outperformance," Vanguard research, July 2013, https://pressroom.van guard.com/content/nonindexed/7.5.2013_The_bumpy_road_to_outperformance .pdf.

2. Ibid., 2.

Chapter 10 Education

1. David Greene, "Education Is Priceless but the Pricetag Is Hefty," *Morning Edition*, May 10, 2012, http://www.npr.org/2012/05/10/152392452/education-is-priceless-but-the-pricetag-is-hefty. Quotes in this section are taken from the transcript of this interview.

2. Steve Odland, "College Costs Out of Control," *Forbes*, March 24, 2012, http://www.forbes.com/sites/steveodland/2012/03/24/college-costs-are-soaring/.

3. Janet Lorin, "College Tuition in the U.S. Again Rises Faster Than Inflation," *Bloomberg*, November 13, 2014, http://www.bloomberg.com/news/articles/2014 -11-13/college-tuition-in-the-u-s-again-rises-faster-than-inflation.

4. Dylan Matthews, "The Tuition is Too Damn High, Part VII—Is Government Aid Actually Making College More Expensive?" *The Washington Post*, September 3, 2013, http://www.washingtonpost.com/blogs/wonkblog/wp/2013/09/03 /the-tuition-is-too-damn-high-part-vii-is-government-aid-actually-making-college -more-expensive/.

5. "Tuition and Fees," Harford Community College, https://www.harford. edu/student-services/paying-for-college/tuition-and-fees.aspx.

6. "Tuition & Costs," Towson University, http://www.towson.edu/main/ad missions/tuitionaid/tuition.asp.

7. "2014–2015 Medical Student Cost of Attendance," Johns Hopkins Medicine, http://www.hopkinsmedicine.org/som/offices/finaid/cost/1415med.html.

8. "Qualified Education Expenses," The Internal Revenue Service, http://www. irs.gov/Individuals/Qualified-Ed-Expenses.

9. Kathryn Spica, "Morningstar Names Best 529 College-Savings Plans for 2014," Morningstar, October 21, 2014, http://ibd.morningstar.com/article/article .asp?id=669116&CN=brf295.

10. Christina Couch, "College 529 Prepaid Tuition Plans at Risk," Bankrate, November 3, 2009, http://www.bankrate.com/finance/college-finance/college- 529-prepaid-tuition-plans-at-risk-1.aspx.

11. John D. McKinnon, "Obama Drops Plan to Raise Taxes on '529' College Savings Accounts," *The Wall Street Journal*, January 28, 2015, http://www. wsj.com/articles/obama-drops-plan-to-raise-taxes-on-529-accounts-1422390991.

12. Chris Guillebeau, "The One-Year, Alternative Graduate School Program," June 6, 2013, http://chrisguillebeau.com/the-one-year-alternative-graduate-scho ol-program/.

Chapter 11 Retirement

1. "Retirement Planner: Full Retirement Age," Official Social Security Website, http://www.ssa.gov/planners/retire/retirechart.html.

2. Jeffrey B. Miller, "$10 Billion in Unclaimed Social Security Benefits," MarketWatch, September 13, 2013, http://www.marketwatch.com/story/10-billion-in -unclaimed-social-security-benefits-2013-09-13.

3. "IRA Deduction Limits," IRS, http://www.irs.gov/Retirement-Plans/IRA -Deduction-Limits.

4. "Amount of Roth IRA Contributions That You Can Make for 2015," IRS, http://www.irs.gov/Retirement-Plans/Amount-of-Roth-IRA-Contributions-Th at-You-Can-Make-For-2015.

5. http://www.irs.gov/publications/p544/ch02.html#en_US_2014_publink1 00072479.

Chapter 12 Financial Independence

1. Anne Tergesen, "Live Long and Prosper. Seriously," *Businessweek*, June 26, 2005, http://www.bloomberg.com/bw/stories/2005-06-26/live-long-and-prosper-dot-seriously.
2. "Health and Retirement Study," University of Michigan, http://hrsonline.isr.umich.edu/.
3. "Holmes-Rahe Life Stress Inventory," The American Institute of Stress, http://www.stress.org/holmes-rahe-stress-inventory/.

Chapter 13 Estate and Legacy

1. "AirTran—Babysitters," YouTube, https://www.youtube.com/watch?v=A Sg9dlhrjEc.
2. Warren Buffett, quoted in Richard I. Kirkland Jr., "Should You Leave It All to the Children?" *Fortune*, September 29, 1986, http://archive.fortune.com/magazines/fortune/fortune_archive/1986/09/29/68098/index.htm.
3. "Estate," The Free Dictionary Legal Dictionary, http://legal-dictionary.thefreedictionary.com/estate.

Chapter 14 Insurance

1. "What Are the Odds of a Shark Attack?" The Wildlife Museum, http://www.thewildlifemuseum.org/docs/content/2113/sharkattackodds.pdf.
2. Josh Sanburn, "Top 10 Oddly Insured Body Parts: Merv Hughes' Mustache," *Time*, September 1, 2010, http://content.time.com/time/specials/packages/article/0,28804,2015171_2015172_2015195,00.html.
3. "Driving While Texting Six Times More Dangerous Than Driving While Drunk," State University of New York at Potsdam, http://www2.potsdam.edu/alcohol/files/Driving-while-Texting-Six-Times-More-Dangerous-than-Driving-while-Drunk.html#.VT5i_q1Viko.

Chapter 15 Life

1. "Check Your Risk," Manulife (risk calculation tool), http://www.manulifesynergy.ca/index.jsp?resourceID=844&Gender=Male&Smoker=No&Age=40.
2. If you're wondering about the impact of inflation on this calculation, there are two reasons why I'm not giving it much mention. First, while we're anticipating a 5 percent withdrawal rate, a diversified balanced portfolio should make more than 5 percent over time, the balance of which goes to offset inflation.
While I realize "safe" withdrawal rates for retirement accounts have fallen from 5 percent to 4 percent (and in some cases even lower), I'm not as concerned about the impact of inflation here because life insurance isn't designed to be a life-long lottery ticket, but a financial bridge to one's future life. If you believe that your situation is one uniquely predisposed to inflation risk, you might consider using a multiple of 20 (instead of 15) and/or using 4 percent as your divisor (instead of 5 percent).

Chapter 16 Disability Income

1. If you make $50,000 per year, instead of $75,000, you would produce $3,770,063 over the next 40 years. If you make $100,000 per year, you would produce $7,540,126 in 40 years. What if you make more but are closer to retirement? Well, if you make $150,000 today, you'll generate more than $7 million in just the next 30 years. If you make $250,000 today, you'll generate $6.7 million in just the next 20 years.

Chapter 17 Long-Term Care

1. "What's Medicare?" Medicare.gov, http://www.medicare.gov/sign-up-cha nge-plans/decide-how-to-get-medicare/whats-medicare/what-is-medicare.html.
2. "What Are the Different Parts of Medicare?" AARP, http://www.aarp.org /health/medicare-qa-tool/what-are-the-different-parts-of-medicare/.
3. "Medicare," LongTermCare.gov, http://longtermcare.gov/medicare-medi caid-more/medicare/.
4. "Benefits Provided by the Federal Long Term Care Insurance Program: Activities of Daily Living," The Federal Long Term Care Insurance Program, h ttp://www.ltcfeds.com/documents/outlineofcoverage/outlineofcoverage_benef itsprovidedadl.html?ooc.
5. Phyllis Shelton, "Long-Term Care Insurance," *Thou Shalt Honor*, PBS, ht tp://www.pbs.org/thoushalthonor/ltc/.
6. Christine Benz, "40 Must-Know Statistics About Long-Term Care," Morningstar, August 9, 2012, http://news.morningstar.com/articlenet/article.aspx?id =564139.
7. "Costs of Care," LongTermCare.gov, http://longtermcare.gov/costs-how -to-pay/costs-of-care/.
8. Kathleen Ujvari, "Long-Term Care Insurance: 2012 Update," AARP Public Policy Institute, http://www.aarp.org/content/dam/aarp/research/public_policy_institute /ltc/2012/ltc-insurance-2012-update-AARP-ppi-ltc.pdf.

Chapter 18 Home and Auto

1. Chris Kissell, "6 Things Home Insurance Won't Cover," Bankrate, http:// www.bankrate.com/finance/insurance/things-home-insurance-wont-cover-1.aspx.

Chapter 19 The Top 10

1. Caroline Ratcliffe, et al., "Delinquent Debt in America," Urban Institute, http://www.urban.org/research/publication/delinquent-debt-america.

Chapter 20 Behavior Management

1. Barbara Roper, quoted in Sheyna Steiner, "How the Fiduciary Standard Protects You," Bankrate, June 19, 2012, http://www.bankrate.com/finance/investing /fiduciary-standard-1.aspx.
2. Ibid.

ABOUT THE AUTHOR

Financial planner, speaker, and author **Tim Maurer**, CFP®, is a wealth advisor and the director of personal finance for Buckingham and the BAM Alliance. Tim writes for *Forbes* and *TIME/Money* and is a regular contributor to PBS and CNBC, where he is a member of their Financial Advisor Council.

A central theme drives Tim's writing and speaking: *Personal finance is more personal than it is finance.* Tim believes that, regardless of our income or net worth, our underlying values and goals drive our behavior with money, which ultimately determines our satisfaction in work and life.

Couching timely application in timeless wisdom, Tim educates at private events as well as in television, radio, print, and online media. With a passion for relational communication, Tim has been featured on CNBC, PBS, and ABC's *Nightline*, on NPR programs *The Diane Rehm Show*, *Morning Edition*, and *Marketplace*, as well as in *The Wall Street Journal*, *The Washington Post*, *The New York Times*, *The Baltimore Sun*, *Kiplinger's Personal Finance*, *U.S. News & World Report*, and *Money* magazine, among others.

Tim is a husband and father first and lives in Charleston, South Carolina, where he and his wife, Andrea, are the proud parents of two boys, Kieran and Connor, and are active members of their community. Outside of personal finance, Tim's favorite pursuit is playing and consuming music. He is also part of a group dedicated to serving the second poorest country in the Western hemisphere, Nicaragua, through microfinance and entrepreneurial ventures.

You can follow Tim at www.TimMaurer.com and on Twitter at @TimMaurer.

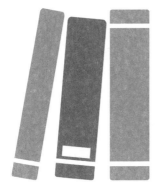

LIKE THIS
BOOK?
Consider sharing it with others!

- Share or mention the book on your social media platforms. Use the hashtag **#SimpleMoney**.

- Write a book review on your blog or on your preferred retailer site.

- Pick up a copy for friends, family, or strangers! Anyone who you think would enjoy and be challenged by its message.

- Share this message on Twitter or Facebook. "**I loved #SimpleMoney by @TimMaurer // TimMaurer.com @ReadBakerBooks**"

- Recommend this book for your workplace, book club, class, or place of worship.

- Follow Baker Books on social media and tell us what you like.

 Facebook.com/ReadBakerBooks

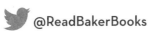 @ReadBakerBooks